WHAT PEOPLE ARE SAYING ABOUT

ANGELS AID

This book provides a beautiful introduction to the power of meditation and the life-changing energy of the angelic realm. Sandra offers clear guidance on how to use the positive energy of the angels to promote well-being, healing and miracles in your life. Sandra has an amazing gift for helping people to connect with their angels and she is the perfect guide for anyone looking to get started with these two powerful practices.

Amy Wall, Lifestyle Editor, *Woman's Way Magazine*

If only all parents had access to this information and would accept it in the non-dogmatic, non-religio it is written! At first I was a little sceptical as to how duce a young child to meditate, but I quickly camditation is really just another way to enconation. All children love to use their imt every day in role play. At least they used I certainly did. Sadly nowadays most 'games' dictated to them by a certain age, by tomputer games and the plethora of TV programmes e for children. They have very little scope to use the power of imagination, which is essential in my opinion. So, this is a very important book because it could if adopted change a generation dramatically. So, even if you don't believe in God or angels or other spiritual concepts in the book, do give the meditations a try. You might be very grateful that you did in a few years' time.

Jenny Smedley, Bestselling author of *Soul Angels*

A wonderful way for children to begin to work with angels of healing...

Angela McGerr, Bestselling author of *An Angel for Every Day*

Angels Aid

Guided Meditation for Children and Parents

Angels Aid

Guided Meditation for Children and Parents

Sandra Rea

BOOKS

Winchester, UK
Washington, USA

First published by O-Books, 2016
O-Books is an imprint of John Hunt Publishing Ltd., Laurel House, Station Approach,
Alresford, Hants, SO24 9JH, UK
office1@jhpbooks.net
www.johnhuntpublishing.com

For distributor details and how to order please visit the 'Ordering' section on our website.

Text copyright: Sandra Rea 2016

ISBN: 978 1 78535 518 9
978 1 78535 519 6 (ebook)
Library of Congress Control Number: 2016941209

A CIP catalogue record for this book is available from the British Library.

Design: Stuart Davies

Printed and bound by CPI Group (UK) Ltd, Croydon, CR0 4YY, UK

We operate a distinctive and ethical publishing philosophy in all
areas of our business, from our global network of authors to
production and worldwide distribution.

CONTENTS

For my two little Princes, Jonathan and Matthew.

Introduction

While being a parent is very fulfilling and rewarding, it can also be tough going at times. I began writing this book after my first son was born. I found meditating and working with the Angels to be a great support during what was an exciting but challenging time. I wanted to share my knowledge so that other parents could benefit also. It quickly became clear, however, that children gain so much from meditation, particularly when coupled with the Angels, which makes the practice so natural and enjoyable for them.

My intention is to help parents to better understand their children, and through meditation give children the tools to become happier, more peaceful and loving individuals.

This book introduces children to meditation in an interesting and enjoyable way through guided Angelic meditations. The meditations are written especially for children to help them to develop and blossom both emotionally and spiritually. Practicing the guided meditations will help your child to sleep better, improve their concentration, strengthen the immune system, encourage healthy eating, and help to bring about emotional balance by decreasing anxiety and promoting relaxation. The Angel meditations are written in a way that you can easily read to your child and teach them to meditate, even if you have never meditated before.

The book is laid out so that each chapter broaches an area of concern, such as behavioral issues, so that you can deal with challenging situations head-on, while also helping your child become more happy and healthy through the practice of meditation.

Each meditation gives a guide to the attributes that it promotes such as better sleep, healing, increased confidence and greater peace or well-being. The meditations can be practiced almost any place and at any time. The intention is to have fun discovering meditation and to enjoy the practice.

You will find that your child will love their meditation time very quickly and will enjoy the bonding time with their parents. The guided meditations can be read at bedtime, during the day before a nap, or at any point to enjoy some stillness and calm.

There is also a section in the book for parents to practice guided meditation if you feel in need of some healing or a peaceful break.

I recommend listening to the sample audio meditation that I have recorded to get an idea of the cadence and flow of the guided meditations. You can then follow the same rhythm when you are reading the meditation scripts out to your child.

The audio meditations are available on my website to download or to order on CD:

www.angelicbodies.ie/angelsaid

Chapter 1

About Meditation and the Angels

What is Meditation?

Many of us have an understanding of the concept of meditation and have heard of its benefits, but how many people actually practice regularly? It seems that the number of people adopting a daily meditation practice is ever increasing, however, there are still many who are aware of the benefits of meditating but never practice. This is partly due to lack of knowledge about how to meditate, the length of time required and the types of meditation.

If we were to learn all of this from an early age and begin practicing from childhood on a daily basis, but in a way that is interactive and fun, we would be more inclined to continue with this beneficial habit into adulthood. And, by the way, there is no particular time requirement or method needed – only a will to meditate, the rest is up to the individual.

So what exactly is meditation?

Certainly, it is the practice of becoming quiet and aware of thoughts; but it is also much more than this. Meditation is the practice of letting go and connecting with your inner self in order to promote peace, balance, self-love and to release negative thoughts and emotions. Through this practice we can also gain an understanding of who we are, our purpose here in life and establish a greater and more meaningful connection with God.

I understand that the mention of God invokes strong feelings in some, and for this reason if you prefer to use another term that feels more comfortable, replace the word God with Source, Higher Power, Creator, Universe or something else that you relate to.

The point is not to get hung up on the term but rather to

embrace the teachings and guidance that this book offers.

What are the Benefits of Meditation?

Meditation has long been practiced over the ages with many attesting to its benefits but it is only recently that we are starting to learn of the scientifically proven benefits that this age-old practice has to offer. Medical studies have now proven the many health benefits of meditation including reduced blood pressure, significantly lowered risk of heart attack, reduced pain and psychological benefits such as less anxiety, emotional stability, greater ability to learn and improved memory and attention. Studies are still examining other benefits of meditation but it is widely agreed that additional positive benefits include a greater sense of peace and balance, improved sense of well-being and a greater ability to cope with stress and challenges that life presents us with.

I equate meditation to a spiritual bath, cleansing not only our physical bodies but our mental, emotional and spiritual bodies also. When we shower and bathe our bodies, we clean away dirt and grime that has naturally built up since we last washed. We all accept that this is a natural process and that regular cleansing is needed in order to keep our bodies fresh and clean. In the same way, meditation when practiced regularly helps to keep our mind and spirit cleansed and refreshed, clearing away heavy energies and dross that naturally build up from day-to-day as we go about our lives. Meditation can cleanse on a deep level getting to the source of issues and helping us to release negativity that has built up over time.

From an early age we teach our children to wash and brush their teeth and to have good personal hygiene. By teaching them to meditate in an enjoyable way, we encourage similar good habits, helping them to understand the importance of mental, emotional and spiritual hygiene so to speak, which is just as important as physical cleanliness. In so doing, you are equipping your offspring with not only the gift of greater peace and happiness but the ability to deal with stressful situations, to handle a range of emotions and to become more centered, balanced and loving individuals. What parent wouldn't want this for their child?

What happens when we meditate?

Initially we will find that our minds can be very active. Thoughts will occupy our minds and it may seem as if we are making little or no progress, but subtle shifts are gradually occurring. For some, even the process of sitting still for ten minutes may at first seem impossible and they may become fidgety or feel an overwhelming need to get up. Others, however, find that straight away they feel more relaxed and at peace.

If you are feeling stressed or very busy, you might find a constant to-do list occupying your mind and may even feel you are wasting precious time when you could be attending to more "pressing" things such as checking your e-mail! Very quickly it becomes easier, however, and as we begin to allow our bodies and minds to fully relax – something few of us ever do – we grow into the practice and start noticing its benefits.

Luckily children don't approach meditation in the same way as adults and are much more open to it. Their attention span is naturally short and this is accounted for in the duration of their meditation practice, depending on their age (more on this below). For the most part, children live in the present and don't feel the same anxiety or pressure to be doing something else. Children immerse themselves in the practice and enjoy what they are doing in the moment.

Fostering this habit early on encourages children to take the healthy practice of meditating with them into later life. Sitting in meditation as a teenager or adult is no longer an alien notion but something that they enjoy and look forward to.

What are the different types of meditation?

There are many ways to practice meditation, which can be a surprise, as some people believe it is just sitting still and emptying the mind. The methods range from mindfulness meditation to guided meditation, transcendental meditation, mantras and forms of motion meditation such as yoga and even walking meditation, amongst others.

While one of the aims of meditating is to become aware of thoughts, it is not the sole purpose of the practice. Where one person prefers to sit in stillness to quiet their mind, another may find it to be more enjoyable to be guided into stillness through listening to instruction and music. Whatever the preferred method, the desired outcome is still the same and it is important to find a process that is enjoyable.

Many people start off trying a number of different types of meditation before they settle on one that they prefer such as mindfulness meditation or transcendental meditation. Ultimately, the method isn't important; what's important is to incorporate meditation into your daily life using whatever practice works for you!

Because children love stories and are great at visualizing, guided meditation works very well. They love to immerse themselves in the meditation and to see in their mind's eye the images and scenarios being described to them. Guided meditation can serve to bring them to a relaxed and comfortable state before bed. Parents often struggle to help their children wind down and relax at bedtime. Meditation is a wonderful way to ease children from playful activity to relaxation and ultimately drifting off to sleep. Children also experience better sleep having practiced meditation than they might otherwise experience. However, depending on the time of day practiced, some of the guided meditations in this book can be revitalizing. Other guided meditations can help in building confidence and self-worth, while some are healing and restorative.

This book is designed to help you to easily select the type of meditation that you wish to practice with your child, with each chapter focusing on a specific area such as promoting sleep, dealing with emotions or healing meditations. As you read the guided meditation with your children, you will also experience some of the benefits that the meditation has to offer. By reading the meditation aloud to your child, you can foster a greater connection with them and a better understanding of the guided meditations. You can also choose to listen along with your children to the audio meditations that I have recorded; to experience the transformative benefits that meditation has to offer, while also spending quality time with your little ones.

How to have fun with meditation

Include meditating in your child's daily routine from as early an age as possible. Children as young as two years will appreciate short guided meditations of two or three minutes.

Let their age be an indicator as to the length of the meditation. Each child is different, but as a guide, use their age to depict the length of the meditation, i.e. two minutes for a two year old, five minutes for a five year old, ten minutes for a ten year old and so forth. If after time they are happy to practice for longer – great, but keep it short to start off.

Allow your child to ask questions during the practice if they feel the need, and don't get frustrated if they start talking or get the giggles as you read. In time they will become more still and learn to relax during meditation, but it is a process that is learned and doesn't necessarily happen overnight. Be patient; don't restrict the child to sitting still or lying down during the meditation. Children are full of energy and love to move about. If they prefer to dance or stand or simply move around during the meditation, allow them to. If children feel that they are restricted to sitting still during meditation time, they will feel confined and will begin to associate meditation with negative emotions.

Let the child be your guide. If they want to practice the same meditation over and over each day rather than trying different ones, go with it. Allow the practice to evolve naturally and don't feel the need to go through the book page by page. Start and stop where you and your child feel happy.

Share your thoughts and emotions with your children after the meditation. Tell them how you felt during the practice and what you liked about it. Your feedback will encourage them to share their thoughts and emotions too. If they prefer not to talk about it, however, respect this also.

Meditation is enjoyable and fulfilling

Meditation offers a peaceful break from the noise and distractions of life. Many children are overscheduled and overstimulated these days, and meditation becomes like a tonic to the soul. Your child will also enjoy spending quality time with Mom or Dad, something that can be sparse during busy family life. As the benefits of meditating begin to develop, you will start to notice a more peaceful, content and loving child if practiced regularly.

Regular practice is the key to receiving the benefits that meditation has to offer; but if you miss a day or two here and there, don't worry, just continue with regular practice when you can.

Angels and Guided Angelic Meditation

Meditation is a spiritual practice and as such it is practiced by many faiths but also by those who do not follow any particular belief system. As we know, Angels are recognized by many faiths and mentioned in numerous religious texts across different beliefs. I mention this to simply point out that there is no conflict with religious beliefs, nor do you have to have any. Regardless of your faith, I recommend keeping an open mind when using this book in order to maximize its benefits and to help your child to enjoy the spiritual practice of guided Angelic meditation.

Why work with the Angels during meditation?

Angels are loving beings of light sent by God to help us on our life path. As we have free will, they can only assist if we ask for their help and invite them into our lives. Although they are always here for us, by our side, they will not interfere with our free will and will only intervene when requested. It is important therefore to constantly ask for their assistance with even the smallest of requests.

During meditation, when we invite the Angels to assist, they enhance the practice in many ways. As we relax during meditation we open up to receiving Angelic help and it can be more powerful than at other times when we might feel stressed for example, and don't really allow ourselves to receive their assistance. Even though we may ask for help during stressful moments, because we have unwittingly built a wall of fear around us, it can be difficult for the Angels to penetrate it. During meditation, this wall melts away and we open up to their love. Over time we learn that we don't need to build a wall of fear around ourselves, and we become beacons of love, easily attracting and receiving our true hearts' desires.

Children in particular identify with Angels and don't doubt their power or their capacity to help us. They love the adventure of meeting their Angels through meditation, and are very open to the experience. They receive enormous benefit from working with their Angelic team of light through their meditative practice.

Children don't see it as unusual or feel afraid of asking their Angels for help, and through Angelic meditation they begin to open up to allowing the Angels to assist in every moment of their lives.

Many children will be familiar with the prayer to their Guardian Angel and will often recite it morning and night:

Angel of God
My guardian dear

To Whom His love
Commits me here
Ever this day
Be at my side
To light and guard
To rule and guide.
Amen

It is a beautiful prayer, and as a child I would find it very reassuring to know that I could recite this prayer and feel safe, protected and supported by my Angels.

Guided Angelic Meditation takes us a step further, allowing children to visualize and meet their Angels; not just their Guardian Angel but other Angels and Archangels too, while also receiving the benefits that meditation has to offer.

Chapter 2

Meeting the Angels

This chapter provides a gentle introduction to guided meditation with some short but effective meditations. I would recommend beginning here and building up to longer meditations detailed in further chapters. I suggest beginning the practice at night before your child goes to sleep when they are tired and already beginning to relax. Although as many of us know, children are not always relaxed at bedtime, and if this is the case, don't worry, practice the meditation anyway, even if they are jumping up and down on the bed! In time you will begin to notice a more relaxed child.

Setting the Scene

Explain to your child what you are going to do. Tell them about meditation explaining that it is like relaxing deeply as if before sleep with their eyes closed but still staying awake and aware of what is going on around them. Make them conscious of the fact that meditation is different from reading a story, as they will close their eyes and see what is being described in their mind's eye. If they prefer to keep their eyes open, however, this is fine too.

When introducing my two year old to guided meditation at bedtime, he lay still, relaxed but with his eyes open throughout. As I finished the meditation, just as I stopped talking, he gently closed his eyes and drifted off to sleep.

Let your child know that even though they are experiencing and visualizing the guided meditation through their mind, what they are experiencing is just as real as if they were to experience the events physically. Tell your child about the Angels and how they will accompany them during the meditation, acting as their guide, protector and friend.

I was finding it difficult to explain to my two year old about Angels in a way that he would understand. Not that children need to understand per se, often they have a better understanding than we do. However, if they are asking questions and would like to know more, this overview is a nice introduction to help them to understand and get to know their Angelic helpers!

While the Angels are often depicted as large and powerful beings – which they are – to children this can seem somewhat intimidating. I prefer to introduce them in a way that children can relate to and feel confident in asking for their help.

Who are the Angels?

Angels are sent to us by God (or "Source" or "The Creator" or whatever term you prefer) to help us. They are beautiful beings of pure light and love. Their purpose is to guide us in our lives to make good decisions, to feel their love and the love of God, to help us to grow and learn, to protect us, to help us to heal when we are sick and to help us in many other ways. All we have to do is ask for their help and they will be there for us. We must always ask first though as we have free will to do as we please. We can choose to invite Angels into our life or we can choose not to ask for their help. They will only help us with requests that are for our greatest benefit and for the highest benefit of others also. The Angels will never do something that might cause harm or upset to someone or something.

What do the Angels look like?

The Angels are the most beautiful beings imaginable. As they are pure light, they can take many forms. They can sometimes look like beautiful stars, shining brightly; at other times they can look like us and we can see their Angelic bodies and hands and faces, but they also have wonderful feathery wings of light. The Angels wear beautiful colors: some wear bright purple and shimmering gold, others wear vibrant green and pink. The Angels are clothed in all the colors of the rainbow and even more unimaginable colors that we can't see. Some Angels wear amazing jewels, others hold gifts and implements in their hands, and some carry instruments to play the most soothing and beautiful music.

What do the Angels do?

As well as helping us, the Angels also look after nature, helping the flowers and plants to grow, they look after cities and countries, planets and solar systems and everything in the universe. There are so many Angels that nothing goes unattended. It is said that for every blade of grass there is an Angel that bends over it whispering "Grow, grow."

The Angels want you to know that you are never alone; there is always an Angel by your side ready to help you when you ask. They are our everlasting guides and helpers, ready and willing to assist. The Angels are overjoyed when we ask for their help, they delight in assisting us and they love when we are open to receiving their loving guidance. We never need to worry when we have such divine assistance always available to us.

Because our Guardian Angels are always with us, we are familiar with their energy and their presence around us, but if we want, we can always ask them to indicate their presence in a way that we will recognize.

Sensing Your Guardian Angel

Sit comfortably and close your eyes.
Take a few deep breaths and relax.
Place your hands lightly in your lap, palms facing up.
Ask your Guardian Angel to tickle your hands with their feathers.

> *Wait for a moment or two to feel the light tickling or tingling sensation in your palms.*
> *It is not uncommon to also feel tickling around your face or other areas of your body such as your feet.*

Now that your child is aware of their Angel's presence, it is time to meet and see them.

Guided Meditation – Meeting Your Guardian Angel
Good for: Intuition, protection, spirituality and confidence
Duration: 2–5 minutes
Best practiced: Anytime
Age Group: 2+

> *Find a quiet place, sit or lie down and relax, close your eyes.*
> *"We ask our Guardian Angels of Love and Light to be here and to connect with us now."*
> *(Pause to feel the presence of your Guardian Angel)*
> *"We ask our Guardian Angels to help us to feel their loving energy around us."*
> *Can you feel the energies of your Angel?*
> *What does it feel like?*
> *(Pause to allow them to feel the energy)*
> *Can you see your Angel beside you?*
> *What do they look like?*
> *What colors are they wearing?*
> *Can you see their wings?*
> *(Pause to allow them to build up an image of their Angel)*
> *Ask your Angel to wrap their wings around you to protect you, feel the loving warm embrace from your Angel as they hold*

you in their beautiful soft feathery wings.

Know that your Angel is always there to protect you and you can call on them at any time to wrap you in their wings.

(Pause)

If you like you can ask your Guardian Angel what their name is. Whatever name comes into your head is the name of your Angel.

(Pause)

You can also ask your Angel a question; whatever is on your mind that you would like to ask them?

When you ask your question, wait for their answer. They may answer you with words or images, or even just a feeling that you get from them. Whatever way they answer is the right thing for you at this point in time.

(Pause to allow them to ask their question and receive a response)

When your Angel has given you their answer they tell you that it is time for you to say goodbye but they will always be beside you and if you want to talk to them at any time.

Thank your Guardian Angel for their help and for everything that they do for you each day.

Feel yourself gently reconnecting with your body.

When you are ready, open your eyes.

Note: No response is needed to the questions you are asking, just allow the child to feel and see the images in their mind's eye. If the child is having trouble feeling, seeing or hearing their Angel just explain to them that it is fine and they don't necessarily need to experience their Angel in these ways at this point in time, and that their Angel is always with them. However, most children will have very vivid images of their Angels.

After the meditation the child may be eager to explain to you what they saw and what messages they received from their Angel. Be open to whatever it is they wish to share with you. However, some children, especially older children, may want to keep the experience for themselves and not want to share with you. This is also fine.

Following on from this meditation, you can spend some time practicing creative activities with your child such as drawing their Angel or painting their Angel's name to hang in their bedroom.

When I practiced this meditation with my two year old, he told me afterwards that the name of his Guardian Angel was Patu Breezy! A few weeks later, we were coloring and I drew a picture of an Angel for him, to which he asked if I had drawn Patu Breezy.

Meeting the Archangels

Archangel Michael

Archangel Michael is a protector Angel. He helps with communication and healing as well as protection. You can call on him if ever you need to say something but you might be afraid to say it or don't know how to explain yourself; he will help you speak easily. You can also ask Archangel Michael for healing, especially if you have had an argument or a disagreement with someone, or if you are in a new place and need his help to make new friends.

He also helps with many other things and if you feel you need his help for something else, just ask!

Guided Meditation – Archangel Michael
Good for: Protection, communication, healing and self-worth
Duration: 3–5 minutes
Best practiced: Morning time, but can also be done during the day
Age Group: 3+

"We ask for our Guardian Angel and Archangel Michael to be here with us now."

Picture Archangel Michael beside you, dressed in blue and carrying a shield and a sword of light. He is tall and strong, and beautiful loving energy comes from him.

You feel very peaceful and protected when he is with you.

We are going to ask Archangel Michael today to protect us and to wrap his bright blue blanket of protection around us.

Picture him with his strong arms placing a beautiful big blue blanket around your whole body and even placing part of the blanket around the back of your head, like a hood.

Once you are completely wrapped in this blue blanket of protection, Archangel Michael gently touches his magical sword on the bottom of the blanket and blue light passes through the whole blanket, lighting up every part of it.

You are now fully protected.

The blanket also gives you healing energy, like a soft warm hug. While you wear the blanket you are always being healed with the loving energy of Archangel Michael.

Thank Archangel Michael for his help and know that you can call on him at any time to help you.

Note: It is beneficial to make this meditation part of your daily practice, placing Archangel Michael's cloak of protection around you and your loved ones each morning.

Archangel Raphael & the Healing Angels

Archangel Raphael works on the Green Ray but also the Gold and Yellow Rays of light. He is best known for healing but is also attributed with energy, harmony, balance and knowledge. He governs over the legions of Healing Angels who assist him with his quest. When we invoke the loving energy of Archangel Raphael, we can tune into his vibration to bring about physical, emotional and spiritual healing for both others and ourselves.

This meditation is great to help with healing when needed; it can also be used to simply lift the child's energy if they are feeling down, or experiencing emotional upset and in need of emotional healing. Also a wonderful meditation for a short time-out to relax and unwind.

Guided Meditation – Archangel Raphael & the Healing Angels
Good for: Physical healing, emotional healing, reenergizing and uplifting
Duration: 3–5 minutes
Best practiced: Anytime
Age Group: 3+

Sit in a comfortable position and close your eyes.

"We ask for Archangel Raphael and the Healing Angels to be here with us now."

Feel the beautiful green energies of Archangel Raphael around you like a soft, warm breeze around your body.

See also the Healing Angels surrounding you, beautiful tall Angels of light helping Archangel Raphael.

Breathe in the loving green light of Archangel Raphael and as you do, feel it enter every part of your body.

Feel the green healing energies in and around your head, your eyes, face and neck.

Feel the energies move down into your chest, lungs, heart and all around your back, shoulders, arms and down around your hips and legs, and see and feel the energies swirling around your ankles and feet.

See every part of your body come alive and sparkle as the green energy passes in and around your body.

Picture any areas of your body that are sore or have been hurt, and see them getting better as the green energy is absorbed into each part of your body that it touches.

If there is any place in particular that is sore or in need of healing, just picture it now as it returns to its full state of health; see the green energy getting brighter and brighter in this area as it intensifies as it heals.

The green light gets so bright that it is almost too bright to look at.

Picture the bright shining green light as it moves into another area of your body that needs to heal.

Follow the light to see where it goes.

It may go to an area of your body that you didn't know needed healing; this is okay, just allow the healing energy to do its work wherever it goes.

The green light may go to two or three places at once, or it may stay focused on one spot.

The light will stay in your body as long as it is needed and will continue to heal you.

Your body is enjoying the extra attention and the healing light as it reenergizes every part of you.

The green healing light flows all around your whole body, bringing a sense of peace as it swirls around and washes over you like ocean waves.

Allow the green light to wash up and down your body, taking any heaviness or any sadness away and replacing it with healing, joy and light.

Know that your body is being healed and energized and will continue to heal.

Thank Archangel Raphael and the Healing Angels for their help.

When you are ready open your eyes.

Archangel Gabriel

Gabriel rules the moon and works on the second Ray of light – the Orange Ray. Although he works on the Orange Ray, he is also associated with white. Working with the feminine energy of the moon, Gabriel helps us to tune into intuition. Combined with logic and heart-based desires, Gabriel can help us to trust and realize our true potential. Angel of the West, Gabriel helps us with emotions and adapting to change. The West is also associated with deepening maturity, introspection and inspiration.

Guided Meditation – Archangel Gabriel
Good for: Imagination, creativity, relaxation and letting go
Duration: 2–5 minutes
Best practiced: Anytime
Age Group: 2+

Sit in a comfortable position and close your eyes.

"We ask for Archangel Gabriel to be here with us now."

Picture Archangel Gabriel as a beautiful tall Angel of silver, white light, with huge white wings.

Archangel Gabriel's clothes seem to shimmer and move

almost as if they are water.

Archangel Gabriel is delighted to be here with you. He takes your hand and you walk with him to a beautiful garden with a large green grassy lawn, surrounded by pretty flowers and trees.

The sun is shining making everything look more beautiful and alive. The heat of the sun warms your body.

You see in the middle of the lawn a pool filled with water. As you walk towards the pool, you see a chair with a swimming costume just for you.

Archangel Gabriel clicks his fingers and suddenly you are dressed in your swimwear.

You smile at Archangel Gabriel, amazed at his powers. He motions towards the pool and you dip a toe in the water.

It is a perfect temperature, and you step in and sit in the clear, warm water.

Floating in the water are gifts just for you.

You see sparkling colorful stones in the pool and as you touch them they change shape and color, almost as if they are liquid, like the water around them.

You stay for a while in the water, exploring gifts around you.

Archangel Gabriel stays by your side and plays with you; he is having fun too.

After a while you decide to step out of the pool.

You have had a wonderful time in the garden with Archangel Gabriel, but you know that it is now time to leave and to say goodbye.

Archangel Gabriel takes you by the hand once again and the two of you leave the garden.

As you arrive back in the present moment, you thank Archangel Gabriel for being with you and for the fun you had.

He smiles and thanks you too.

Ariel

Ariel isn't traditionally known as an Archangel, but I've included her here as we'll be working with her in many other meditations in upcoming chapters. Ariel is associated with the elements of earth and air. A beautiful, multifaceted Angel, Ariel's energy is powerful and transformative. Ariel brings grounding energy with the element of earth but also lightness of being with the element of air. She reminds us of our creative abilities and helps us to bring about that which we desire, helping us to believe we deserve to achieve our true hearts' desires.

This meditation can be done in the garden or in nature to maximize its benefits, but it is also very effective if practiced indoors.

Guided Meditation – Ariel
Good for: Creativity, uplifting, healing and confidence
Duration: 5 minutes
Best practiced: Outdoors, anytime
Age Group: 3+

Sit in a comfortable position and close your eyes.
Take a few deep breaths.
"We ask for Ariel to be here with us now."
Feel the light energy of Ariel around you as she comes to you on the breeze.
Feel her tickle your face and hands with her kisses.
Feel her all around you and as a part of you as her breeze passes through your hands, your hair and through your whole body, into your lungs, your heart, your arms and legs, and swirling all around you.
See her purple, blue energy as it swirls around you, always moving and changing color, bringing healing to every part of

your body.

Ariel invites you to become part of the wind with her; as she takes your hand your body transforms into the breeze and you fly with her through the air.

You pass through and around trees, feeling their leaves and branches tickle your face as you fly.

You blow through the grass, feeling each blade of grass run through your fingers as you pass.

You rise up into the sky, and your breath blows the clouds through the air.

You fly towards the sea and with a lick of your tongue you create huge waves that dance and sparkle in the sunlight, and as the water splashes back into the sea you feel the spray from the waves splash your face and body.

As you fly along the beach you see people enjoying themselves and you lift kites into the air with a touch of your hand as you breeze through.

You fly towards a small forest and you creep through the trees gently rustling the leaves that have fallen to the ground as you glide by.

The air is refreshing and you feel light as you fly along, leaving any heaviness or worries that you were holding onto behind you.

Ariel brings you back to the point where you started and brings you back into your body.

She kisses you gently and flies off on the wind, yet she still remains all around you and within you.

You thank her for the wonderful adventure and for the healing.

When you feel ready, open your eyes.

Archangel Uriel

Archangel Uriel works on the Ruby Red Ray, however, like the flames of a fire, his colors transform from vibrant red to yellow, orange and gold. Archangel Uriel's name means "fire of God" and he is thought to reflect the inconceivable light that is God. Ruling over the element of fire, Uriel is connected with transformation, creativity and balance. However, this illusive Archangel also brings us the gifts of understanding, spiritual devotion, knowledge, determination, focus and transmutation with his fire of life.

Guided Meditation – Archangel Uriel
Good for: Connecting with nature, grounding, empathy and peacefulness
Duration: 5–10 minutes
Best practiced: Anytime
Age Group: 3+

Sit in a comfortable position and close your eyes.

"We ask for our Healing Angels of love and light and Archangel Uriel to be here with us now."

Picture Archangel Uriel standing beside you as a beautiful golden, orange being of light.

Archangel Uriel's presence is very powerful but also very loving and light.

Feel his energy around you.

Feel the strength of his wings as they enfold you.

Archangel Uriel wraps you in the warmth of his loving energy.

Spend a few moments to relax in his love.

Archangel Uriel explains that he sends beautiful sunshine to nourish nature.

He takes you by the hand and brings you to a magnificent rainforest where the trees are so big that you can't see the top of them, and their trunks are so large that you could step inside them.

The forest radiates beautiful, green healing energy. Everywhere you look there are different shades of green, from pale green leaves to deep dark green moss.

The whole forest seems to be alive and you soak up its vibrant energy.

There is a pathway before you, and with Archangel Uriel by your side, you walk deeper into the huge forest.

You see beautiful butterflies and birds along the way with rainbow color feathers and their sweet song is like no other bird's you have heard before.

You smile as you look into the trees and see these beautiful birds flying about.

Suddenly you fly up into the trees, like the birds, and you land at the top of one of the tallest trees. Sitting on a bed of leaves, you look out over the forest.

The sun is shining down on you and it feels warm and peaceful.

As you look out over the tops of the trees, you can see the forest for miles all around you.

Occasionally you see a bird flying out of the trees and up over the forest.

The energy of the forest is replaced by stillness, a quiet stillness that you have never felt before but it also seems so familiar to you.

You close your eyes for a moment to bask in the peace surrounding you.

Archangel Uriel tells you that this forest is very special, and that the energy from the rainforest helps to give life to the whole world and that the forest is alive and breathing and has a soul.

Your presence in the forest and your appreciation of its beauty helps the forest to survive.

You realize that you are a part of all living things and their energy is in you, just as your energy is a part of them.

You breathe in the clear fresh air and the energy of the forest into your body, knowing that everything is as it should be.

Archangel Uriel tells you that it is time to leave the rainforest but that it will always be a part of you, and in reality you are never separated from it.

You feel yourself back in your body and in the present moment.

Thank Archangel Uriel for the experience and thank the forest for the healing.

When you feel ready, gently open your eyes.

Chapter 3

Chakras

A book about meditation and Angels wouldn't be complete without an introduction to the energy system and the chakras. There is so much that could be written on this subject alone that it would require a separate book, but in order to understand how the energy field operates, this introductory guide will enable you to have a basic understanding of its functions.

What exactly is a Chakra?

The word chakra is derived from the Sanskrit word meaning spinning wheel. This is a good analogy as the chakras are swirling vortices of energy, very much like swirling liquid. Each chakra is cone shaped, emanating about a foot out from the physical body. There are seven major chakras, which are situated at points along the body, as described in the following chakra overview. There are also numerous minor chakras located at various points throughout the body.

The chakras or energy centers assimilate and feed energy along energy lines or meridians to the physical body and within the aura; much like oxygen being distributed through our circulation system. This complex system of energy centers makes up the energy field or aura.

It's important to understand how the energy system works in order to gain a greater insight into the benefits of guided Angelic meditation and how imbalances in the energy field can lead to behavioral issues or illness. Often we put "bad" behavior down to stubbornness or just being bold, but children never misbehave just for the sake of it; there is always an underlying cause and often it can be a plea for help on their part if they have been ignored and have exhausted all other means of communication.

So how does this relate to the energy system? When we experience emotions, we feel them around certain parts of the body; for example, we sometimes describe sadness as heartache. These emotions are also experienced through our energy centers – the chakras.

Take another example: when we are excited and feel butterflies in our stomach, what we are experiencing is actually the energy build up in the third chakra – the sacral chakra. Each chakra has different attributes and functions and if – as mentioned above – a child is constantly feeling ignored or not worthwhile they also experience this through their sacral chakra. An ongoing feeling of being unworthy can lead to energy in this chakra becoming stuck, and if it is not cleared, this feeling of unworthiness can be carried into adulthood. In some cases, the cycle is repeated through attracting relationships – be it friendship or romantic – where the individual again experiences feelings of not being worthwhile.

This emotional blockage can often be resolved, however, through guided meditation, bringing the chakra back into balance and functioning as its optimal level.

Chakra Overview

Root/Base Chakra
Location: Base of the spine, in the pelvic area
Attributes: Peace, confidence, balance, focus, courage and energy
Color: Red
Flower: Red Rose

Sacral Chakra
Location: Below the naval

Attributes: Self-worth, creativity, vitality, expression and wisdom
Color: Orange
Flower: Orange Lily

Solar Plexus Chakra
Location: Above the naval
Attributes: Power, strength, confidence, sense of humor, self-esteem and optimism
Color: Yellow
Flower: Sunflower

Heart Chakra
Location: Center of the chest
Attributes: Love – love for self and others, happiness, peace, compassion and empathy
Color: Green and pink
Flower: Water Lily

Throat Chakra
Location: Base of the neck
Attributes: Communication, expression, speaking and being true to oneself
Color: Turquoise blue
Flower: Blue Pansy

Third Eye Chakra
Location: Center of the forehead
Attributes: Intuition, inner knowing, self-assurance, imagination and foresight
Color: Indigo or purple
Flower: Indigo Iris or Purple Violets

Crown Chakra
Location: Top of the head
Attributes: Spirituality, wisdom, oneness and divine power
Color: Violet or white
Flower: Purple Lotus Flower or White Lily

Breathing Exercise

This breathing exercise can be done on a regular basis with your child as a fun activity. It will teach them to control their breathing, release anger and become centered. It can be a useful tool to help children manage anger. The key is to practice the "game" when they are in good form, and not just when they are getting frustrated and angry.

Place two *pencils or crayons on the floor or on a table in front of you and your child. Explain that you are going to play a game to see who can blow the pencil the furthest.

Ask your child to take a deep breath in, saying: on my count take a deep breath, one, two, three, breathe in, breathe in, breathe in, now hold...

Pause for a second.

Now blow! Breathe out, breathe out, breathe out... Keep blowing out for as long as possible.

As you are blowing out, the pencil should roll across the table. Repeat the game for as long as the child is interested!

This will help your child to practice deep breathing.

Next time you feel your child is getting angry or frustrated try this game. It will not only act as a distraction, it will also help them to release frustration through deep breathing.

Note: If you are not at home or in a situation where it is not possible to set up a pencil just start by saying: take a deep breath, one, two, three, breathe in, breathe in, breathe in, now hold and blow... If they are used to playing the game they will know what to do.

*For older children you could add more of a challenge to the game by using a feather. Place the feather on the child's lips with their head tilted upwards, ask them to blow the feather into the air and to keep it up for as long as possible!

Color Breathing

Once your child has mastered deep breathing as explained in the previous exercise, they can start to develop the healing breath of life by using different breathing techniques. This will benefit them enormously and help them to regulate their emotions, rather than displaying emotional outbursts, ultimately bringing about greater balance and well-being.

This exercise can be done at any time but it is a great way to relax before sleep.

Color breathing uses the colors of each of the main energy centers or chakras to balance and heal each chakra.

Guided Meditation – Healing Breath of Life
Good for: Healing, grounding, peacefulness and relaxation
Duration: 5–10 minutes
Best practiced: Anytime
Age Group: 3+

"We ask the color Angels to be present and to connect with us now."

Imagine floating up amongst the clouds. You are floating

along with beautiful, vibrant, rainbow colored clouds.

First, you hop onto a red cloud.

See this bright red cloud all around your body. This is a special cloud that sparkles and shimmers.

You smell roses within the sparkling red mist; you smell their lovely scent not just with your nose but also through your whole body.

Start to take a deep breath in, see the beautiful red mist entering your body.

See it filling up your whole body with red sparkles – your head, your neck, your shoulders and arms, your chest and back and even into your blood and organs; see it filling up your tummy and your hips and legs, and flowing down through each foot.

(Allow your child to take a few deep breaths in and out of the beautiful red energy, healing and balancing their Base Chakra.)

Now see yourself floating onto the next cloud of bright orange.

As you step into the cloud, you are surrounded by beautiful orange mist.

You smell and taste oranges, not just with your nose and mouth but you smell and taste them through your whole body.

Take a deep breath in; see the orange mist becoming part of your body.

See the beautiful orange cloud filling up your whole body, your head, your neck, your shoulders and arms, your chest and back and even into your bones and muscles; see it filling up your tummy and your hips and legs, and flowing down through each foot.

(Allow your child to take a few deep breaths in and out of the beautiful orange energy, healing and balancing their Sacral Chakra.)

Now see yourself floating onto the next cloud of brilliant yellow.

As you step into the cloud, you are surrounded by beautiful yellow mist.

You smell and taste sweet lemons, not just with your nose and mouth but also again through your whole body.

Take a deep breath in; see the vibrant yellow mist coming into your body.

See the beautiful yellow cloud filling up your whole body, your skin, your head, your neck, your shoulders and arms, your chest and back; see it filling up your tummy and your hips and legs, and flowing down through each foot.

(Allow your child to take a few deep breaths in and out of the beautiful yellow energy, healing and balancing their Solar Plexus Chakra.)

Now see yourself floating onto the next cloud of green and pink.

As you step into the cloud, you are surrounded by beautiful green and pink mist.

Take a deep breath in; see the bright green and pink mist flowing into your body.

See the beautiful green and pink cloud filling up your whole body, your hair, your head, your neck, your shoulders and arms, your chest and back, your heart and lungs; see it filling up your tummy and your hips and legs, and flowing down through each foot.

(Allow your child to take a few deep breaths in and out of the beautiful green and pink energy, healing and balancing their Heart Chakra.)

Now see yourself floating onto the next cloud of sky blue.

As you step into the cloud, you are surrounded by beautiful blue mist.

You hear and smell the ocean, you feel as if waves of blue water are massaging your body.

Take a deep breath in; see the blue mist flowing into your body.

See the beautiful blue cloud filling up your whole body, your hair, your head, your neck and throat, your voice, your shoulders and arms, your chest and back; see it filling up your tummy and your hips and legs, and flowing down through each foot.

(Allow your child to take a few deep breaths in and out of the beautiful blue energy, healing and balancing their Throat Chakra.)

Now see yourself floating onto the next cloud of purple.

As you step into the cloud, you are surrounded by vibrant purple mist.

Take a deep breath in; see the purple mist flowing into your body.

See the beautiful purple cloud filling up your whole body, your forehead, your face, eyes and ears, your neck and throat, your shoulders and arms, your chest and back; see it filling up your tummy and your hips and legs, and flowing down through each foot.

(Allow your child to take a few deep breaths in and out of the beautiful purple energy, healing and balancing their Third Eye Chakra.)

Now see yourself floating onto the next cloud of pure white.

As you step into the cloud, you are surrounded by glistening white light.

Take a deep breath in; see the white sparkles flowing into your body.

See the beautiful white light filling up your whole body, your head, your brain, eyes and ears, your neck and throat, your shoulders and arms, your hands and fingers, your chest and back; see it filling up your tummy and your hips and legs, and flowing down through each foot and your toes.

(Allow your child to take a few deep breaths in and out of the beautiful white light healing and balancing their Crown Chakra.)

Now see yourself floating onto the last cloud of gold.

As you step into the cloud, you are surrounded by sparkling golden light.

Take a deep breath in; see the golden glitter flowing into and around your body.

See the golden energy forming a gold egg of protection around you.

As you sit within this golden light, you know that you are always protected and loved.

Feel yourself back in your body, still surrounded by this protective golden bubble.

"Thank you, color Angels, for helping."

Chakra Colors & Chakra Mantras

A mantra is a word or phrase that is used during meditation to focus the mind. The mantra can be spoken aloud by chanting it or simply repeated silently in the mind. The purpose of the mantra is to allow your focus of attention to be brought back to the mantra each time you have noticed the mind wandering.

This meditation is a powerful and soothing way to balance and realign the seven major chakras. The chakra colors used combined with the frequencies of the chakra mantras have a powerful, healing and restorative effect. Chakra mantras are tones or sounds that vibrate at the same frequency as the related chakras.

However, if the chakra is blocked or misaligned then the frequency may be disrupted. Repeating the chakra mantras can help the associated chakras to respond to the tone, bringing its vibration back to the desired frequency (a bit like a tuning fork). If practiced on a regular basis this meditation will promote peace, well-being, balance, vitality and positive emotions.

As children are very visual, they will love imagining the chakra colors in and around their body while also having fun repeating the mantras.

Note: Repeat each mantra a number of times for each chakra. The number of repetitions can be altered as desired. Chant or sing the mantras with your child so that it becomes a fun joint activity.

Base Chakra – LAM
Sacral Chakra – VAM
Solar Plexus – RAM
Heart Chakra – YAM
Throat Chakra – HAM
Third Eye Chakra – SHAM
Crown Chakra – OM or AUM

Guided Meditation – Chakra Mantras
Good for: Balance, focus, healing, well-being and positivity
Duration: 3–5 minutes
Best practiced: Anytime
Age Group: 3+

Sit or lie in a comfortable position and close your eyes (if the child prefers, they can also choose to stand for this meditation).

Imagine red light in and around your feet, legs, thighs and hips. This red liquid light flows all around and through your legs and hips.

This is the color of your base chakra, located at the base of the spine.

The sound associated with this chakra is LAM.

While imagining the healing red light, breathe out fully, take a deep breath in and chant – LAM, LAM, LAM (repeat a number of times before moving onto the next chakra).

Next imagine beautiful, vibrant orange light around your tummy and lower back.

This is the color of your sacral chakra, located below the belly button.

The sound associated with this chakra is VAM.

As this orange light flows in and around your body chant – VAM, VAM, VAM...

Next, picture bright yellow light around your waist and back.

This is the color of your solar plexus chakra, located above the belly button.

The sound associated with this chakra is RAM.

See the yellow light flowing around you saying – RAM, RAM, RAM...

Now, imagine deep, grassy green light around your chest and upper back.

This is the color of our heart chakra, located in the center of the chest.

The sound associated with this chakra is YAM.

See the light changing from green to pink and flowing all around you, chanting – YAM, YAM, YAM...

Next, imagine clear, sky blue light around your shoulders and neck and mouth.

This is the color of your throat chakra, located at the base of the throat.

The sound associated with this chakra is HAM.

See the blue light flowing in and around you and say – HAM, HAM, HAM...

Next, see beautiful purple light around your face, forehead and back of the head.

This is the color of your third eye chakra, located in the middle of the forehead.

The sound associated with this chakra is SHAM.

As the purple light flows around your head and face, chant –
SHAM, SHAM, SHAM...

Last of all, bring your attention to the top of your head, and imagine pure white light at the very top and just above the head.

This is the color of your crown chakra, located at the top of the head.

The sound associated with this chakra is OM (pronounced AUM).

See the white light swirling around the top of your head saying – OM, OM, OM...

Repeat for as long as desired.

Note: The mantras don't have to be repeated in succession and not all of them have to be done together. If you choose to, you can focus on just one mantra such as Om.

Chapter 4

Healing

When our children become sick, we can sometimes feel powerless to help them with the healing process, other than to allow them the time and rest to get better. However, the restorative effects of meditation can aid their bodies' natural healing process.

Meditation is known to strengthen the immune system, help reduce inflammation, reduce pain and to provide a host of other health benefits that are currently being discovered and researched. In addition to the healing effects of meditation, it is also a powerful preventative practice that over time and with repetition can help to maintain health.

Of course illness and pain does also serve a purpose, for example, when babies begin teething, it is usually their first experience of pain. The purpose of this, apart from the obvious purpose of growing teeth, is to help their spirit or soul to connect into their body on a physical level, which the pain of teething can contribute to and help with the process.

When we consider a time that we experienced pain, we are very present in the pain, in the present moment. It is a powerful way to focus our energy and attention. It is almost impossible to concentrate on other tasks when we are in severe pain, let alone think about the past or plan future events. We are focused in the moment. Children go through a series of grounding phases where their spirit connects more deeply with their bodies during each phase. Teething is the first level which can occur over a series of phases, often months apart. After which, other phases can come about through sickness or emotional pain where each time the child connects more with their body and this earthly reality through pain and emotions.

It can sound like a harsh reality and we may wish to protect our children from such events but we are not helping them to move forward by preventing such occurrences. Even if we did succeed in preventing the child from experiencing pain from teething, for example, it can't be completely avoided and it would most likely come back in another form.

That said, not all illness serves to ground the child spiritually, and some children can suffer unnecessarily from bouts of pain and sickness from environmental influences or even take on the pain and suffering of a family member which can then present itself through the child as illness. Our children hate to see family and loved ones suffering from stress, fears and worries, and can try to alleviate our unease by taking on the burden themselves energetically. Ideally, our role is to help them through times of pain or illness that are necessary for their growth and help them to avoid unnecessary suffering and disease.

That's not to say that we are helpless and must watch on as they experience such events. We can allow the process to occur in a more easy way and often over a shorter time period if we are aware of what is happening and have a few tools on hand to help the process along.

It is never easy for a parent to see their child suffering; our natural reaction is to protect and shelter our offspring from danger and harm. Once we understand, however, that we are all here to learn and to grow spiritually we can adopt a better understanding of the life experiences that our children and we must go through. We have all come into this life with a knowledge of life lessons and challenges that we must face in order to evolve. By understanding and accepting this, we can choose to sail through life's challenges rather than resisting them, which only creates far more pain and suffering. In the same way, we can teach our children how to cope with and flow through challenges without resistance, helping them to learn and integrate their life lessons in an easier way.

We have already met Archangel Raphael and the Healing

Angels. In this chapter we will continue to work with them as well as other Angels who can help our children to recover from illness, ease pain and maintain health.

Guided Meditation – Releasing Pain & Illness
Good for: Healing, release, restoring balance and relaxation
Duration: 10 minutes
Best practiced: Anytime
Age Group: 3+

If your child is feeling ill or is going through a difficult situation, they will benefit enormously from this meditation.

> *Close your eyes and imagine yourself surrounded by Healing Angels.*
>
> *Your body is able to heal itself if allowed to.*
>
> *This meditation will activate your body's healing abilities allowing you to easily return to full health and balance.*
>
> *Picture in your mind one cell from your body as a circle with a dot in the center. It is not a perfect circle as it is slightly wobbly, and it is always moving and wobbling about.*
>
> *What color is this cell?*
>
> *Now imagine that there are millions of these cells throughout your body, making up your skin, hair, blood, heart, bones, and all the tissues of your entire body.*
>
> *All the cells are moving and wobbling about.*
>
> *Take a moment to picture a dog that has just been washed and is soaking wet. It stands up and starts to shake its body to shake the water off. Its fur raises off its body as it is shaking and the water flies off in all directions.*
>
> *Now imagine that you recorded the dog doing this but played it back in fast-forward so the dog is moving and shaking even*

quicker than before.

Picture once again one of your cells, the wobbly circle with a dot in the center. The cell starts to wobble faster and shake like the dog was shaking the water off, except it is moving ten times faster than the dog even when he was speeded up in fast-forward!

See anything inside the cell that might be causing sickness or pain being shaken out of the cell, like the water easily flew off the dog.

You will notice a blue light surrounding the entire cell and anything that comes out of the cell is caught by this blue light and transformed into blue light also.

Now imagine that every single cell in your body starts to shake faster and faster, shaking off anything that doesn't belong in each cell, and being collected by the blue light surrounding your entire body.

You will start to feel a tingling sensation moving from your feet all the way up through your body or maybe starting in your tummy and moving out, down your legs and arms and up through your head.

Allow this ripple of energy to pass through you. It may even pass up and down your body a few times getting faster and faster before it finally eases off.

Once the feeling has stopped you know that your cells will continue to shake at a faster speed than normal but you no longer have a tingling feeling.

You can practice this again any time you want to let go of hurt or pain.

Take a deep breath and open your eyes when you are ready.

Note: This meditation may need to be practiced a number of times depending on the illness or situation before it is fully released on a physical level. Other healing may need to be done on an emotional and spiritual level to help the child to completely heal. Further guided meditations in this chapter and in Chapter 5 can be practiced in conjunction with this one.

Ariel – Healing Breath

Ariel governs the elements of air and earth. As well as helping to regulate the air in our environment, Ariel can help with healing, in particular in relation to breathing issues related to asthma and clearing blocked noses or sinuses for example. We can also ask Ariel to help cleanse and clarify the air in our home or workplace to ensure we are getting a clean, fresh supply of oxygen. Ariel is also great at transmuting and cleansing our energy field and the energy in our homes.

This healing meditation is intended to help children suffering from breathing issues but it can also be used at any time to help refresh their energy.

Guided Meditation – Healing Breath
Good for: Breathing easily, connecting with nature, healing and peacefulness
Duration: 10 minutes
Best practiced: Bedtime or when needed
Age Group: 4+

Sit in a comfortable position, close your eyes and begin to relax.
"We ask for Ariel to be here with us now."
Feel the light, breezy energy of Ariel in and around your body.
Her energy is so soft; it is barely noticeable unless you are very still and relaxed.
Welcome her into your space and into your energy field saying:

"Ariel, please be with me now and help to clear away any blockages or restrictions to my breathing. Help me to breathe freely and easily and to sleep well this evening. Please also be with me during my sleep to continue to allow my airways to remain clear and unrestricted."

Take a few deep breaths and feel the energy of Ariel entering your body as you breathe in.

See her energy as a beautiful purple, pink and blue color as you breathe it in.

As her cleansing, healing and restorative energy flows in and around your body, see it clearing any areas that are blocked and feel the release that this brings to you.

Continue to breathe in the beautiful purple, pink and blue energy of Ariel, allowing it to completely heal and refresh your body in whatever way that is needed.

See your body filling up with this purple, pink and blue light and feel any burdens or heaviness being lifted from you.

Allow yourself to let go, knowing that you are completely safe and protected.

Spend a few moments in this energy, and if you want to ask Ariel a question, ask it now and listen for her response.

She may answer you in words that you hear inside your head or through an image that you see or even a feeling that you get.

Thank Ariel for all her help and know that you can ask her to be with you at any time you feel she is needed in your life.

Note: If your child is too young to do the above meditation you can ask for Ariel's assistance on their behalf. When my son was a baby, if he had a cold, I'd often ask Ariel to help with his breathing when putting him to bed. The following invocation can be said on behalf of the child:

Ariel, please be with <NAME> now and help to clear away any blockages or restrictions to his breathing. Help him to breathe freely and easily, and to sleep well this evening. Please also be with him during his sleep to continue to allow his airways to remain clear and unrestricted.

Releasing Pain

This meditation is beneficial to help ease pain. It is also useful for relaxation and healing even if there is no pain or illness present.

We will work with Archangel Raphael, the Healing Angels and Archangel Michael to provide healing and relief from pain through this guided meditation. Even if the child is asleep or in a remote location, the meditation can be recited on their behalf and they will still receive the benefit.

Guided Meditation – to Relieve Pain
Good for: Pain relief, teething and relaxation
Duration: 5 minutes
Best practiced: Anytime
Age Group: Any age

Begin by calling in the Angels.

"I ask for Archangel Raphael, the Healing Angels and Archangel Michael to be present and to connect with me [or NAME] now."

Wait for a moment for the Angels' energy to connect with you.

Picture yourself in a forest filled with healing energy. The light from the sun filters through the trees and provides sunshine and warmth.

You are safe in this space and you feel peaceful and at ease.

You sense the presence of the Angels; and as you look around, you see the green healing light of Archangel Raphael and the Healing Angels in every space around you, the green leaves and pine needles, the grass and moss, and even in the air all about you.

The birds are singing and their song also brings healing to you as they sing beautiful songs.

The forest, the air and the songs of the birds bring you into a state of deep relaxation and healing, promoting your natural healing frequencies.

As you walk deeper into the forest, you feel yourself becoming more refreshed, healthy and balanced with each step.

This is a magical place; and as the soft breeze flows through the trees and around you, you hear the whispers of the Angels on the wind. They are telling you how much you are loved and how you are perfect in every way.

Their words heal you on an even deeper level and you begin to let go of any burdens or heaviness that you once felt the need to carry inside of you.

This is a place of balance and joy, and as you relax, you become in tune with the harmonious energy of the forest.

Your body, mind, emotions and spirit all become balanced and aligned with your surroundings.

Looking ahead, you see an opening leading out of the forest.

Just before the opening you see the wonderful, tall, blue shape of Archangel Michael as he greets you with his beautiful smile. As you walk up to him, you immediately feel at ease around him.

You notice that he is holding a magical sword made of blue light and a protective shield.

He blesses you with his sword of light, protecting you from harm before you leave the forest.

Michael also wraps a blue cloak around you and you feel its supportive protection envelop you.

You leave the forest feeling safe, protected, healthy and peaceful.

Chapter 5

Emotional Ups and Downs

Helping our children to deal with their emotions is a vital part of parenting. Emotions are not necessarily a bad thing, but we as parents can get upset if we see anger or sadness or frustration expressed in our children. We believe that part of our job is to shelter them from negative emotions and experiences, and help them to live happy lives. While this is a noble pursuit, it is not necessarily of benefit to them.

We all come into this life knowing that we will experience a range of emotions and challenging situations. If we did not have this contrast we would not learn and grow during our lifetime. We would remain one-dimensional so to speak.

Different emotions and situations help us to experience a range of feelings and events that we can learn from. If we were to constantly experience sunny weather, we wouldn't appreciate the sunshine as much. We would take it for granted, seeing and feeling the same thing every day. We'd also miss out on the beauty and awe of a thunder and lightning storm or the magnificence of snow, and all the range of weather conditions that bring us such variety and splendor.

In the same way, our emotions serve us in various ways. The key is to be able to observe the emotions subjectively, to learn from them, without getting caught up in feelings of blame, guilt, fear, pity or judgment, of both ourselves and of others.

When we engage with negative emotions such as anger or fear, we can become caught up in them, unable to release the emotion and missing out on the lessons that they have to teach us. We can also store this energy in our bodies for prolonged periods, sometimes leading to sickness if not released. If we allow the emotion to flow through us, however, we can observe and learn from it.

Children are actually very good at letting emotions flow, crying one moment, laughing the next and then angry or frustrated, all within a short space of time. The reason for this is that they allow themselves to experience the emotion fully as it arises; but instead of holding onto it and analyzing it as adults tend to do, they release it as quickly as it arrived. This is good!

When we see strong emotions arising, however, in our children we can react negatively. It can also awaken our emotional bodies leading us into negative emotional patterns in response. If we then try to control or limit the child's emotional behavior this can in turn lead to a strong reaction from the child often in the form of more negative emotions. It can all be quite overwhelming.

If we take a step back we can see what is going on. Children are emotional beings, just as we are, and they have a right to express their emotions. When we respond by telling them to stop being bold or to stop behaving that way, we try to suppress their emotional reaction. This leads to frustration and a feeling of being misunderstood. We haven't tried to assess the source of the emotion; we only reacted to the behavior.

Before reacting, if we ask the child what happened or why are they upset and give them a chance to explain, we will not only understand their behavior better but we will teach them that it is okay to express emotions and that we will not judge them for it or try to overpower their behavior. We can also help our child to work through an emotion when we recognize it and help them to understand their feelings.

This meditation is designed to help us and our children release pent-up emotions that we might be holding in our bodies unnecessarily. Allowing for this release can also help them to feel better and to react in a more subtle way the next time the emotion arises. For example, if a child has much frustration and anger in their emotional field, this will be expressed sometimes strongly and frequently, as it is present on a surface level. Once released, they no longer need to engage with this energy, and as a result the frequency and severity of the frustration or anger that's expressed decreases.

Guided Meditation – for Emotional Release
Good for: Balance, emotional release, healing and intuition
Duration: 5 minutes
Best practiced: Anytime
Age Group: 4+

Take a deep breath in.

Begin to tune into your body and ask it how it is feeling.

Wait for a response. This might come in the form of words or feelings in a certain area of your body, or just an overall sense of knowing.

What emotions are coming up? Is there happiness and love, or do you sense any anger or sadness or some other feeling?

Whatever is coming up, know that it is okay to experience this without judging the emotion.

Where is this emotion located in your body?

Can you see this emotion as a particular color? It might look like bright vibrant light or it could be more like a dull grey color or something else that comes to mind.

Whatever comes up is okay.

See yourself surrounded by Angels.

They are holding what looks like cleaning utensils – a feather duster, a vacuum cleaner, a mop and some other items.

The first Angel holding the vacuum cleaner comes over, they smile at you and you feel very safe and welcome. The Angel very gently starts to suck away painful emotions that are now ready to be released.

You know that the emotions being released have served their purpose, and it is now time to let them go and move on.

The Angel works quickly, and before you know it they finish vacuuming and another Angel comes over with a feather duster to finish cleaning this area. They smile as they work and you feel very happy with their attention and care.

Another Healing Angel comes over with a small bag filled with gold dust. They begin sprinkling this beautiful golden dust onto the area that was cleaned and all over your body.

As the dust lands on your skin, it lights up very brightly before being absorbed into your body.

As you look down you see that the area they were cleaning is completely cleared and is glowing with a beautiful golden light.

Thank the Angels for their help and know that you can ask for them to help you in the same way whenever you are feeling angry or sad or fearful.

Say goodbye and feel yourself back in the present moment, feeling refreshed and happy.

Controlling Children's Emotions

As adults we can get irritated when our children express emotions of anger, frustration and sadness. We have been conditioned to suppress our emotions and believe that our children should do the same. In fact, it is wonderful that they can be so expressive and show their emotions with such ease. The difference between the ways they show emotion compared to adults is how they can let go so easily. The emotion passes through them and it is gone. Anger is released in seconds and replaced with joy, and sadness is followed by laughter.

Rather than trying to change the way our children express themselves, we should embrace their openness and follow their example.

It is tempting when we see a child throw a toy on the floor in anger to say, "Don't throw things, that's bold." What we could say instead is, "I can see you are frustrated, that's okay, do you want to talk about it?" Or something along those lines, something that acknowledges our child's feelings and tells them that it is natural to feel and to show emotion but that there are other options also. We can also ask them why they are feeling that emotion at that time, for example, "I can see you are frustrated, what happened to make you feel that way?" Let them explain and congratulate them for being open, "Well done, it's great to explain how you feel and to understand why you are feeling that way." If the child is too young to talk you can still ask these questions. They might not be able to answer but they will begin to understand that showing emotion is good and that talking about it and being open is a great way to express themselves. When you ask the question, pause and then answer for them. For example, "I see that you are frustrated, what happened? Did your Lego break and you felt angry and frustrated? Will we rebuild it together?"

Soon they will learn that rather than throwing something in frustration, they can instead explain, "I'm angry because I wanted to play with my Lego but it fell apart."

Once we know why our child is angry we can talk to them in a more open way, and understand the source of their emotions.

Anger is often feared and showing sadness, crying for example, can be seen as a sign of weakness, particularly in men, but these are all part of our makeup; they are integral to our being, just as positive emotions of love, happiness and peace are too. Suppressing these emotions causes them to become bottled up, building inside of us only to be released with greater vigor in an outburst of anger or floods of tears. But this is still better than not releasing them at all. I believe that when strong emotions are held inside without an outlet, they can cause pain and illness.

Think about it, if you are holding onto anger or any other

"negative" emotion within your body for extended periods of time, this energy can damage your physical being in the form of disease or conditions such as depression. Equally, if you infuse your being with emotions of love and happiness then you will encourage health and well-being.

The key is to be childlike and to let go of emotions as they arise, allowing them to pass through us but without dwelling on them, and to encourage our children to do the same – not to suppress their feelings.

Children & Free Will

Often as parents one of the main things that we struggle with is conflict of will. You want your child to sit still and eat their dinner; they want to play, feel the texture of the food with their hands, throw the food about and do everything else but eat it! This is their natural desire to explore and learn. While it might be amusing one day when you are feeling patient, it can become irritating when it happens every day at every mealtime.

This is just one example of a conflict of will between you and your child; but as we all know, this happens in numerous other circumstances and repeatedly throughout the day. It can be very frustrating but it is also teaching us valuable lessons of patience and understanding.

In order to put things into perspective place yourself in your child's shoes. Imagine you decided to go out for a walk, it's a beautiful sunny day and you open the front door to leave your house. As you open the door you take in a deep breath of fresh air and you feel the warm sunrays touch your face. Suddenly, your partner pulls you back inside the house and shuts the door, saying angrily, "No, you can't go outside." Imagine how you would feel – frustrated, angry, bewildered... You try again to open the door and the same thing happens. Now you are really feeling angry but you can't talk so you have to express your anger in another way, by grunting and pushing your partner away and perhaps crying. You can't understand why they won't let you do what you want to do.

What you don't realize is that they want to go out for a walk with you too but they have to finish a task that they are in the middle of before they can join you. If at the start your partner explained their intentions the situation would be very different. "I want to come out for a walk with you but I can't go at this moment as I am in the middle of an important task. I'll be finished in ten minutes and then we can go together."

It may seem silly explaining things like this to your child, particularly when they are very young, but you'd be surprised at how much they can understand. You are also treating them with respect and recognizing that they are a person with their own free will and intentions. It is a good habit to adopt early on as it won't be a big change to make when your child is a bit older and can understand you better and even reply to you.

You will find that there are times when you forget to explain your intentions and why you are doing something, and this is to be expected. With practice it gets easier and it will become a habit. The important thing is to try not to be too hard on yourself if you forget and return to old ways from time to time. You can always apologize to your child saying something like, "Sorry if I shouted at you (or was impatient), I'm just feeling frustrated but it is not your fault. I will try to be more understanding in the future." It is important for the child to know that your reaction isn't because of them and they are not to blame. You might be thinking, well, actually my reaction was because of something that my child did! However, external incitements, which bring up feelings of anger, frustration, sadness and so forth, are not the cause of these emotions but rather the stimulus that brings forth the emotion. You can always choose how to feel and how to express your emotions. For example, if you have a headache and your child is playing and making a loud banging noise, this may aggravate your headache and you might come to a point where you shout at your child saying, "Stop that awful noise." On the other hand you can choose to react in a different way explaining, "I have a sore head and the noise is very loud, why don't you play with this other toy for a while." You have explained the situation to them and you have given them an alternative option to resolve the situation.

You will find that once you start talking to your child in this way, they will respond back in the same way, explaining their emotions and why they are doing something. You will have a more open and understanding relationship with your child. If you decide to communicate in this way, it is important to explain this to all family members, so that they too can adopt this behavior. Be sure to encourage them when they are practicing expressive communication and, equally, if they slip up from time to time don't be harsh with them. It is a learning process for all the family.

Emotional Healing

Life can be quite frustrating as a child. Trying to express yourself, being denied the things you want, not understanding what's going on and having to do things that you don't want to do. As discussed previously, our children are individuals with their own personalities, and they want to express their free will and to be their own person. When their self-expression is repeatedly denied, naturally they can become frustrated and emotional.

In order to help our children to process and release built-up emotions, the following meditation not only allows for this release but also surrounds the child with beautiful emotional healing energy.

Guided Meditation – for Emotional Healing
Good for: Emotional balance and healing
Duration: 5 minutes
Best practiced: Anytime
Age Group: 3+

Sitting comfortably, relax and close your eyes.

"I ask the Angel Camael and Angel Phuel to be with me now."

See and feel the beautiful energies of the Angels as they surround you with emotional healing, light and love.

Breathe in deeply and see the light from the Angels being drawn into your body.

Breathe in this light through every part of your body and feel the restorative benefits as the light heals your emotional body.

You might feel a sense of comfort or a sense of peace as all your worries melt away and your emotional body is filled with healing light.

Continue to breathe in this revitalizing, healing light. With each breath feel the comfort and support of the Angels Camael and Phuel filling you up, filling every part of your body with light.

As the energy builds, you feel a deep sense of peace and happiness as any weight or burdens that you have been carrying around are lifted.

You happily surrender these burdens to the Angels, knowing that there is no longer any need for you to hold onto them.

As the Angels continue to surround you in light, you hear a beautiful voice telling you that you are loved unconditionally, that you are beautiful in every way and that you are safe and protected in their loving care.

Take a while to rest in this healing light and to absorb the energy the Angels are sending to you.

When ready, thank the Angels Camael and Phuel for the healing and feel yourself reconnecting with your body in the present moment.

Changing Negative Behavior to Positive Behavior

After our children are born, we begin very early to notice their unique characters and disposition. As they grow, we may refer to them as being "spirited" or "shy" or other descriptive words to describe their characters. However, when we refer to them in this way, we are only identifying one very small part of their complex personalities and ultimately limiting them and ourselves through this narrow viewpoint.

When we repeatedly describe them in this way, not only do we begin to expect them to display these personality traits, they too begin to identify with these limiting descriptions. As children always want to please their parents, they will even begin to act in the way that we describe them to be (whether true or false) just to please us and reflect back the characteristics that we have come to expect.

The problem is that when a child has displayed unwanted characteristics and we begin to describe this and tell others that the child is "bold" then this behavior is also amplified, even though this is far from the behavior that we want to see and experience as parents.

When we develop preconceived opinions of our children's personalities, we unwittingly affirm this behavior and come to expect it, to the extent that when it is displayed it is reinforced each time: "There he goes again, such a bold boy."

In order to release the child from these restricting notions, we first need to let go of them ourselves. Generally we attract what we focus on in life, and if we concentrate on bad behavior or timidness or other such characteristics as the main element of our child's personality, then this is what we will receive.

Releasing ingrained beliefs can be difficult to do, especially if this behavior is what we are constantly being presented with. The key is to be ever present and vigilant of our thoughts and opinions. Once we make a decision to change our thinking, then we need to hold strong and be aware of our new thought processes in order to change old thought patterns.

How can we ever expect our children's behavior to change for the better if we are not even able to change our own thoughts and behavior?

Once we have decided to release ingrained thoughts and opinions (this is not something that happens overnight, it is a constant practice from minute to minute), we then need to also change our reactions. Instead of immediately reacting to the behavior our child displays, stop and observe them and say nothing where possible. If it's a case that the child is in danger of hurting themselves or others, then we obviously need to intervene, but where possible don't react immediately. Wait until the impulse reaction has passed and then choose how you wish to respond. For example, if your child hits you with their hand or one of their toys, which is usually a means to get your attention, instead of saying, "No, don't do that, it's bold," pause, stay silent for a moment and then decide how you wish to respond. Bring yourself back to a place of love and then respond. Perhaps hold their hand and say, "I love you, I know that you don't mean to hurt me but when you hit me like that it is very sore, please be gentle." While saying this, if they are holding an object such as a toy, gently take it out of their hands and put it aside. Follow up by asking them if they want to tell you something or do something with them. If they do have something to tell you, listen to what they have to say and talk to them. If they ask you to do something such as play with them, if possible make the time to play, even if only for a few moments. This will reinforce positive future behavior and show your child that they don't need to misbehave to get your attention. If it's not possible, explain that you do want to play but it's not possible now, and give them a specific time when you will play such as after lunch or in ten minutes rather than just saying later, which to them usually means never!

Once we have decided to release our ingrained thoughts and change our behavior and reaction to our children's behavior, the third element is to develop new beliefs about them. If you view your child as being shy, instead take time to visualize them behaving in a confident and friendly manner towards others, chatting easily and enjoying other people's company. Feel grateful for their natural confidence and ability to express themselves. Spend time each day visualizing their new positive behavior and ideal qualities, and experiencing the feelings of joy, gratitude and peace that it brings to you. Also reinforce this image of your child by telling them that they have a great personality, they are so confident and self-assured. Describe them in this way when you meet other people so that they hear you telling friends and family the same thing.

Their behavior may not change overnight; but with persistent and consistent practice changing your own behavior and thought processes, you will start to notice positive changes in your child.

Guided Meditation – to Release Worries
Good for: Releasing sadness, worries and fears
Duration: 5 minutes
Best practiced: Anytime
Age Group: 3+

Picture yourself in a sunny open space in nature. This could be a beautiful field filled with flowers, a forest, a hill or mountain, or another place that comes to mind.

Feel the heat of the sunshine on your body.

You feel very safe and welcome here.

Spend some time exploring the area. Look around you. Admire the beautiful flowers and smell their sweet scent.

You come across a pathway and begin to walk along it.

You are greeted on this path by Angel Camael who is here to help you.

He takes you by the hand and leads you to another area off the pathway.

As you look ahead, you see a magnificent white horse with a beautiful flowing mane and tail.

As the horse comes over to greet you, you realize that it's a unicorn. It gently nuzzles your neck; its whiskers and soft hair tickle your skin.

Camael asks if you would like to sit on the unicorn and you immediately say yes, knowing that there is nothing to fear.

Angel Camael sweeps you up and places you on the unicorn's back, and you grab hold of its long mane.

As you look around, you can see much further, now that you are higher up than before, and you admire the fabulous view all around you.

You notice some birds soaring high in the sky and some butterflies in the grass.

In the distance you see some deer wandering through a meadow.

It is very peaceful.

You also feel connected with the unicorn, and as you sit on its back, you can sense the power and life force of the animal.

Camael sits on the horse also, just behind you, gently holding you in his arms.

You feel powerful, free, at peace and loved.

You ask the unicorn to take you someplace and you begin to feel its legs moving beneath you, at first walking and then gaining speed.

As the unicorn moves faster, you feel the breeze in your hair and it seems to blow away your cares and worries.

With each step the unicorn takes you feel lighter and happier.

You pass through fields and along hillsides, through forests and by rivers, all the time moving at speed.

You sense that the unicorn moves with the wind and it is part of and one with nature.

After some time, you begin to slow down, and the unicorn brings you to a lake and stops to take a drink.

You and Camael jump off the unicorn and dip your hands and feet in the clear, fresh water.

You splash some water on your face and it feels cool and refreshing.

You sit with Camael by the side of the lake and watch some birds as they float on the water.

The sound of the water is soothing and you feel that this is a special place; a sanctuary created just for you to enjoy.

The unicorn comes over to say goodbye and again nuzzles your neck before leaving.

Talk to Camael and tell him anything that is on your mind.

Listen to the advice that Camael has for you and thank him

for being with you.

As you get up to leave you find yourself back on the pathway that you started out on.

Camael hugs you and waves goodbye.

You feel yourself back in your body and in the present moment.

Chapter 6

Healthy Eating

If we could see the energy and vibrancy of the plants, fruit and vegetables that we eat, our meals would take on a whole new dimension. We would see the energy and vitality in and around fresh, natural food, and the lack of this vital energy in processed foods. We'd appreciate how this energy is assimilated and absorbed by our bodies and put to good use. We would also recognize how much energy we expend digesting processed food, receiving little energy and nutrients in return.

If our diet consists mainly of processed, unnatural food, we are using more energy digesting the food than we are getting from it. It's no wonder that so many people are lacking in energy and constantly feel tired.

This meditation takes children on a journey, allowing them to see the vibrancy that organic, unprocessed food provides and seeing how this is absorbed into their bodies.

Guided Meditation – to Appreciate Food
Good for: Healthy eating, appreciation, imagination and curiosity
Duration: 5 minutes
Best practiced: Anytime
Age Group: 2+

"We call on Angels Ariel, Sofiel, Isda and our Guardian Angels to be with us now and to guide us in this meditation."
The Angels greet you and tell you that they are going to take you on a journey.

Your Guardian Angel takes your hand, leading you down a pathway.

The path is surrounded by lush, green grass, and as you near the end you see a field filled with plants, fruit trees and vegetables.

You step off the path onto the moist soil and look all around you.

As you look around at the beautiful fruit trees and vegetables, you see apples, strawberries, pumpkins, beetroot, lettuce, cucumber and potatoes growing under the soil.

Your Angel points out some herbs and flowers that you can eat as well as some giant watermelons and a plum tree.

Everything seems to grow here in harmony.

As you delight in the bountiful scene, your Angel waves their hand before your face and you begin to see the energy light up inside the fruit and vegetables.

Sofiel pulls up some carrots from the ground and you notice sparks of yellow, orange and red light inside and around each carrot.

The light moves and dances and is very beautiful.

Sofiel cleans the soil off the carrot and hands it to you to taste.

As you put it into your mouth, you can feel the sparks of light dancing around your tongue. It feels nice, and the flavors of the carrot are sweeter and more flavorsome than you have ever tasted before.

As you finish chewing, the light and energy from the carrot enter your body as you swallow, and looking down at your body, you can see the light inside you.

It sparkles red and yellow and gold as it's digested by your body and is absorbed by your cells.

The light radiates out from your tummy to the rest of your body – your legs and arms and you feel a warm glow inside of you.

You spend some time with the Angels tasting all sorts of fruit and vegetables.

Each has their own special colored light dancing inside and around them.

The strawberries have red and pink and white light, the beetroot has beautiful deep red, purple and golden sparkles, the lettuce holds vibrant green, yellow and white energy.

The whole field becomes alive with the dancing energy and light from the fruit and vegetables.

Each bite tastes better than the one before and your body lights up with the colored energy of the fruit and vegetables that you are eating.

The Angels are also dancing around the field and tasting the wonderful flavors that the fruit and vegetables have to offer.

Your Guardian Angel returns to you with a basket filled with amazing fruit and vegetables for you to take with you as a gift.

You gratefully accept the basket, and the two of you turn back towards the path to leave.

Isda tells you to close your eyes for a moment each time you eat to see the dancing light inside the food you are about to taste and to give thanks for the energy that it provides.

As you arrive back in your body, you feel refreshed and energized.

Guided Meditation – to Appreciate Nutrition
Good for: Healthy eating, creativity, imagination and wonder
Duration: 5 minutes
Best practiced: Anytime
Age Group: 2+

"We ask Angels Uriel, Isda and Sofiel to be here with us now."

We ask the Angels to take us on a guided trip into and through our bodies to help us see where the food we eat goes and how it helps our bodies.

See the Angels take you by the hand and see yourself step outside of your body. You start to become smaller and smaller until you are barely visible.

You and the Angels go back into your body through your mouth, the same way the food you eat goes in.

You see yourself in your mouth, standing on your tongue; it's warm and wet, and a warm breeze blows past as you breathe.

You look around at your teeth and at the roof of your mouth, and you smile at the Angels standing beside you as you look forward to the adventure that lies ahead.

You look towards the back of your mouth, and with a quick run and a big jump you are sliding down your throat.

You slip down a long tunnel until, pop: you land in a large cave with a pool in the middle.

You sit with the Angels beside the pool watching all that is going on. It is a very busy place...

Lots of workers are busily cleaning and hammering and going about their jobs.

Right beside you a worker is hammering what looks like a rock. The rock cracks open and reveals what seems to be sparkling diamonds.

The worker is very happy; he picks up the diamonds and carefully carries them off to be used in another part of your body.

It's time to move on, and you and your Angels dive into the pool at the center of the cave, as it starts to swirl around and drain out through the bottom of the cave, a bit like water draining from the sink.

You swirl around and around, and before you know it, you find yourself landing in a green field.

As the liquid from the cave rains down around you and lands on the moist earth, the grass seems to become energized from the moisture as it is absorbed into the earth.

You pause for a moment, standing looking up with your hands raised in the air as you feel the rain on your skin.

The green field is also filled with workers, some so tiny that they are hidden in the grass and some much bigger who seem to be lifting and moving heavy objects.

The little workers in the grass are tending to the soil and lifting out stones and things that are not meant to be there.

One worker near you has filled a wheelbarrow full of pebbles and stones, and she happily wheels it off to another area.

There is a lot happening around you and you would like to join in.

Angel Isda points to a rocky area and tells you that you can help the workers to break down the rocks.

A worker hands you a hammer and chisel, and you start to tap away at the biggest rock.

Little pieces fly off as you hammer and they land on the ground around you.

As soon as they scatter on the ground, another worker arrives and sweeps them away.

The rock that you are working on breaks up quite fast, and is gathered up by the many workers around you.

You ask Angel Isda where they are taking the rubble and you both follow the workers wheeling away the rocks into a tunnel.

The workers are wearing hard hats with lights attached to the front so that they can see down the dark tunnel.

The walls of the tunnel sparkle in the light and you see one of the workers from earlier placing the diamonds that he found into the tunnel walls where they are needed.

As you walk along you see a worker with a feather duster cleaning the tunnel.

Another worker is holding a hose and spraying water all around the tunnel.

The tunnel splits into two and you follow it around to the right where it seems to grow bigger.

There is a lot more going on in this tunnel and everyone seems very busy.

The workers are singing as they go about their jobs, moving and shifting rocks and rubble.

They seem to be really enjoying their tasks.

A loud horn sounds, toot, and everyone stands aside.

Suddenly the rocks and rubble start moving down the tunnel as if by magic and they disappear out of an opening.

The workers are very happy that all their hard work has paid off. They have a short rest before it is time to start again.

Uriel tells you that there is so much more to see, but that's all there is time for on this visit.

You run with the Angels towards the opening that the rocks went through, and with a giant jump you leave your body and return to your normal size.

When you reach your full size you step back into your body.

You thank the Angels for their help and for showing you how your body works.

> *You realize how important it is to eat healthy food to help the workers in your body to do their jobs and to keep your body working properly.*

Chapter 7

Nurturing Positive Characteristics

Promoting Self-Esteem and Confidence

The use of our language towards ourselves and towards our children is so important when it comes to building our children's self-esteem and confidence. If your child, even if only a baby, constantly hears you saying things like, "Silly Mommy," when you do something wrong or even worse, "Stupid Mommy/ Daddy," they will learn that you don't value yourself and that it's okay to put yourself and others down; even if only in jest. We mistakenly think that if we say something jokingly then it is not offensive or doesn't have meaning: "It was just a throwaway comment."

On the contrary, everything we say whether seriously, mockingly, sarcastically or otherwise, has the same impact; there is no differentiation by means of the tone. If you say something or someone is silly, you are little by little chipping away at the self-esteem of that person even if unintentionally. Always speak of yourself with the utmost regard, not in a boastful or conceited manner but in a way that demonstrates respect and pride for yourself. Equally, always speak of your loved ones, friends, acquaintances and everyone that you encounter in this way. It teaches your children by example and they in turn will learn to speak highly of everyone they meet, including themselves.

I often hear parents call their child a "silly billy" when the child falls over or drops something. It was on the tip of my tongue to jokingly say "silly billy" so often when my first child was born; I really had to make an effort not to say it, and to keep silent or to say something positive instead.

When our children are developing their motor skills, learning how to walk, talk and interact with their environment, it's a big learning curve and so amazing how much they learn and so quickly.

When we consider, most babies are born so helpless and small, and usually within a year they are walking, communicating, attempting speech and a variety of other skills. It is natural that they learn through trial and error, as we all do, and it's essential for us to praise their efforts, even if it doesn't work out on the first, second or even third attempt. Next time if tempted to utter the phrase "silly billy," or something worse, reconsider your language. Pause and then say something else such as, "That's okay, let's try again," or "You're doing great, let's start over."

It can be difficult at first to change your thought and speech patterns but it is possible, and with conscious effort it becomes natural over time.

I am always conscious to praise and promote my children's efforts, using descriptive praise to acknowledge what they are doing or not doing, as is often the case!

If you find that you have been prone to using negative phrases towards yourself and your children, fear not. You can begin to readdress your habits and start to promote positive self-esteem with this guided meditation. And if you do lapse from time to time, this is natural. We can negate a negative comment by immediately saying something positive. So if you accidentally say, "Oh you're a silly billy," and realize just as you're saying it, you could follow up with something positive such as, "You're so wonderful" or something along those lines. The important point is to maintain your efforts and keep practicing.

Self-Love

In order to receive love from another, we must first appreciate self-love. When we love ourselves and everything about us – even the perceived negative aspects – we shine our light and open up to accepting love from those around us. The following meditation will help children to develop and deepen love for themselves, drawing more love from others into their life.

Guided Meditation – to Love Oneself
Good for: Self-confidence, love, harmony, peace and self-worth
Duration: 5 minutes
Best practiced: Anytime
Age Group: 5+

Sit in a comfortable position. Close your eyes and take a few deep breaths.

"We ask for the Angels of love and self-worth, Amabiel and Haniel, to connect with us now and to assist with this meditation."

The Angels are going to take you on a journey of self-discovery.

They are going to allow you to see yourself through their eyes and God's vision of you.

The Angels take you by the hand and bring you back to a time when you were younger.

They show you a scene from your life when you were very happy with your family, and enjoying their company and their love for you.

It could be the moment when you were born. Being held lovingly in your parents' arms, or it could be a time of celebration such as a birthday party and there is lots of laughter and fun. Or it could be another time in your life when you felt very loved by your family.

Whatever scene comes up, spend a few moments exploring it and seeing it from all aspects – from your own point of view, from your mother's eyes, your father's eyes and even from your brother's and sister's eyes.

Feel the joy and love that each person is experiencing.

Now look around and see all the loving Angels that were present with you during this moment.

See the love they have for you and see how they are helping to enhance the love that you have for each other.

The room is filled with loving energy and you can even see the energy as it moves about and between each person, and the exchange of loving light.

It is wonderful to experience this moment once again.

After a while, the Angels take you by the hand and bring you to another scene in your life.

This time it is a moment when you felt unloved or abandoned by someone in your family.

You might have felt that you were at fault and that you were not good enough.

Your Angel shows you the other person's perspective.

They bring you back to a moment in this person's life, earlier that day when they felt stressed or tired and brought those emotions with them to the encounter with you.

The Angels show you that even though the person allowed these negative emotions to get the better of them, it was not because of you or something that you did or didn't do that caused the emotion.

They show you deep inside this person's heart and the flame of undying love that they have for you, a love so strong that it never burns out or dies; it continues on into infinity, and no matter what you do that love will always exist.

You feel the emotion of love coming from this person and it touches your heart.

Your Angel shows you inside your own heart and you see the flame of love inside you growing ever stronger as it is healed.

You let go of whatever masks were covering your heart and you allow your flame of love to shine.

It shines so brightly that your chest lights up, brighter than the sun.

The rays of your love shine out for all to see and feel.

You do not need to be overwhelmed by the power and the emotion of your love, as this is your natural state.

It has always been inside of you and will forever continue to grow stronger.

Now that you have opened your heart, you will receive back tenfold the amount of love that you give out. The love will come back to you many times stronger from your family, friends and from all the people you encounter every day.

The Angels bring you back to your body and seal in the love.

They tell you they are always here to help and they are delighted that you are opening your heart. You will go on to do great things in your life and this is only the start for you.

Thank your Angels, and when you are ready, gently open your eyes.

Fostering Self-Worth

Generally, children have a strong sense of self-worth from a young age. When exposed to other people's opinions – parents, teachers or other children – they can begin to develop self-doubt and question their worth, however. Often we are taught that we have to earn approval from our parents or teachers by behaving in a certain way. If we are "good" or do well at school we get rewarded, but if we are "bad" we get punished. Pretty soon we learn to conform to the expectations of others to fit in or to avoid disapproval. This is sad because along with conforming, we lose some of our essence, our sense of wonder, play, creativity and self-worth.

We can, however, help our children to keep these virtues alive, and to value themselves and the valuable contribution that they offer the world. We can nurture their sense of worth by being less critical and less judgmental of their actions, which can sometimes mean allowing them to make mistakes along the way but learning valuable lessons from their efforts. As is often said:

It is better to try and to fail than to fail to try and forever experience the inestimable loss of what might have been.

We can also allow our children to awaken their curiosity, creativity and sense of wonder and self-worth through meditation. When practicing guided meditation, the key is to develop not just their ability to visualize but to immerse themselves in the practice with all of their senses – tasting, touching, hearing, smelling and seeing what is being described in the meditation. Not only does this help to open up their creative centers, they also begin to trust their own judgment and their ability to be creative and inventive, fostering a greater sense of worth and value.

If your child describes the imagery and events that took place in a guided meditation, always listen with interest, being open to what they are describing without saying that it wasn't real or was just imaginary. Dismissing their meditation as being something that is not real defeats the purpose of the practice, and could dissuade the child from further practice or from being open in describing their experience.

In this meditation your child receives a gift from their favorite Angel. They are given something special just for them to keep. They are worthy of this special gift and there are many other gifts that will be given to them by God and the Angels; they just have to know that they deserve them and be open to accepting them.

Guided Meditation – to Foster Self-Worth
Good for: Self-worth, confidence, self-belief and assurance
Duration: 5 minutes
Best practiced: Anytime
Age Group: 3+

We'll begin this meditation by asking our Guardian Angels to help and also calling on your favorite Angel to be by your side.

You might know the name of your favorite Angel, and if you do, say their name three times, and ask them to be with you now.

If you don't know their name, just picture the colors of this Angel and see them standing beside you.

This Angel has a blessing for you.

They place their loving hands gently on your shoulders and they say a prayer to God. They are asking for you to know your worth, and how significant and important you are. They ask God to shine light on you to allow you to see how magnificent and loved you truly are.

You see a ray of beautiful golden light beaming down on you and you feel the love, peace and happiness that the light contains.

You feel a great sense of love and you know that you are part of this loving energy, and that you can spread this love to others by shining this loving light out from your heart to each person you meet.

This loving light holds great power, which you respect, and you feel honored to be part of this special experience.

As you stand in this light, your favorite Angel steps forward holding out their hands. Their wings are spread out behind them and you sense their great power and love.

Looking into their hands they open them up to reveal a beautiful object, a special gift just for you.

As you admire and take in the beauty of this gift, your Angel reaches out towards you and you lift your hands to gratefully receive this wonderful present.

Taking the gift into your hands, you take a moment to admire it before bringing your hands towards your chest and the magical gift is absorbed into your body, becoming part of you.

You know that this gift serves a purpose, and when the time is right it will be there for you to help you in many ways.

You know that you too, along with every other person on Earth, have a very special purpose in life, one that you will enjoy carrying out when the time comes.

For now you trust that your Angels are always by your side, helping you as you continue to learn and grow, and preparing for your important life purpose.

You sense that it is time to leave. As you return to your body, you take the special gift and the light of God with you, holding them inside of you.

You thank your favorite Angel and your Guardian Angel for their help.

When ready take a few deep breaths and open your eyes.

Guided Meditation – Sending Love
Good for: Love, balance, healing relationships, self-worth and relaxation
Duration: 5–10 minutes
Best practiced: Anytime
Age Group: 4+

"We ask the Angels Amabiel and Haniel to be here and to connect with us now."
Picture yourself in a special healing place surrounded by

beautiful pink Angels of love. This can be a place outdoors in nature or a room you feel very safe in such as your bedroom.

The Angels are sending beautiful, bright pink healing light to you.

Allow yourself to soak up this pink healing energy and to feel the love coming from these Angels.

Picture someone that you love, it could be your parents or a brother or sister or friend.

Feel the love that you have for this person.

See little pink love hearts coming out of your chest and floating through the air towards this person; as they float along, they grow in size and the power of your love for them grows too.

See these love hearts containing your love for this person reaching them and swirling all around them before popping open, sparkling as they touch the person and showering them in your loving energy.

You smile as you see the person you love filled with joy as they receive your loving energy.

You see them place their hands on their heart, and as they extend their hands out towards you, beautiful pink love hearts start to float out from their chest to you.

You laugh as you feel the power of their loving energy coming towards you, and you see the love hearts growing bigger and more loving as they float through the air.

As they swirl around you a large heart passes in front of your face; you can see inside the heart its beautiful, colorful, sparkling, loving energy and you are amazed at the beauty within.

As the hearts gently touch your body, they pop and the glowing, loving energy showers you in love.

You celebrate and enjoy the warmth of this love that you are receiving.

> *Thank this person for their love and thank Angels Amabiel and Haniel for their help, knowing that you can return at any time and send love to any person in your life.*
>
> *You feel yourself gently returning to your body, bringing the love that you have received with you.*
>
> *When you feel ready, open your eyes.*

Note: This meditation is a very powerful way to restore balance in any relationship and is especially helpful if the child has a person in their life that they are having a tough time with. For example, in a case of bullying, the child can picture the person that is bullying them and send them love as detailed above. It is helpful if the child has first carried out the meditation picturing a person that they love so they can relax and really feel the power of the love they are receiving.

Do Only What You Love

Everyone has been made for some particular work, and the desire for that work has been put in every heart.

~ Rumi

Children already have within them all they need to be, to do or to become whatever they want. Whether a sports player, physicist, singer, philosopher or writer, the options are endless. This innate talent just needs to be nurtured. It will come about at the right time. We as parents often think, "I wonder what my child will be when he/she grows up." This sentence in itself is flawed, as children don't have a desire to be anything (apart from the learnt desire to be something or someone), they just want to do what they love. Besides, when do children actually grow up? Do we ever reach a milestone where we can say, "Today I am now an adult"? No, and we wouldn't want to, as each of us holds within us an inner child that never dies. If our inner child did die, wouldn't it also be the end of our sense of fun, play, laughter and innocence? Since we are always learning and growing, we can never claim to have grown up!

Guided Meditation – The Magical Garden
Good for: Connecting with nature, creativity, grounding and balancing
Duration: 5–10 minutes
Best practiced: Anytime
Age Group: 4+

Find a comfortable position either indoors or outside and close your eyes.

"We call on the Angels Sofiel, Achaiah, Aratron and Hahlii to be present and to connect with us now."

Picture yourself in a beautiful garden, filled with flowers.

The colors of the flowers are so bright and beautiful and they seem to beam their colors out at you.

You feel the heat of the sun on your face, and as Angel Hahlii points up into the blue sky, you notice a beautiful rainbow.

You turn to face one of the flowers nearby and lean towards its petals breathing in its wonderful smell.

As you admire this flower, you notice that curled up in the center of the petals is a tiny fairy, fast asleep.

You smile at the sight and stand for a moment watching this cute little fairy.

Suddenly the fairy starts to wake up, and as she lifts her head, she shakes off some pollen in her hair and looks up at you.

Without saying any words, you realize that the fairy is talking to you, and she tells you that she is glad to meet you and is delighted that you are here in this beautiful garden.

The fairy explains to you that all of the flowers are homes to many other Angels and fairies and they look after the garden.

She also tells you that the garden has special healing powers, and that just by being there you are being healed and reenergized.

The fairy reaches her hand out towards you, and as you take her hand, suddenly you start to get smaller and smaller until you are the same size as the tiny fairy and you are standing beside her on the petals of the flower.

She wants to take you around the garden and to show you many special things.

Little wings suddenly appear on her back as if out of nowhere, and she takes your hand again and the two of you fly off around the garden.

She stops and lands on a giant mushroom at the bottom of the garden; she explains that this is a shaded quiet place that the Angels and fairies of the garden can come to sit and read.

You both jump off the mushroom onto the moist earth and you see that there are beautiful colored crystals hidden below the mushroom.

The fairy tells you that you can pick a crystal to take with you. Looking at the crystals, you choose the one that you think is most beautiful.

As you place it in your pocket, the fairy once again takes you by the hand and you both fly off to visit another part of the garden.

You notice that you are flying towards a small pond in the corner of the garden.

The pond is filled with beautiful pink water lilies floating on giant green leaves.

As you fly down to the pond, you land on the water and you realize that you and the fairy are so light that you can walk on the water.

The sight of a pretty dragonfly in the air above catches your eye and you notice how its clear wings seem to take on different colors as it flies.

The dragonfly lands beside you in the pond and asks you your name. As you reply, you are delighted to be so close to the dragonfly, and to be able to see its beautiful wings so clearly and to admire the colors that they take on.

The fairy tells you that it is time to move on and takes you by the hand again. You say goodbye to the dragonfly as you fly off with the fairy.

You fly over the garden once again and a beautiful, tall sunflower catches your eye.

Its yellow petals are so pretty and soft and the center of the sunflower is filled with pollen that the bees are collecting.

As you and the fairy land in the center of the sunflower, you are dusted in the yellow pollen but it doesn't make you sneeze and you both laugh.

You sit for a while watching the bees coming and going, collecting pollen from the flowers to make honey.

You can hear birds singing in the garden; they sing the most beautiful songs, like no other birdsong that you have heard before, and the fairy tells you that they are singing just for you.

The songs make you happy and give you feelings of peace and joy.

You realize that it is time to leave the garden but the fairy tells you that you can come back whenever you want to and there is a lot more that she wants to show to you.

You hug the fairy and thank her for the wonderful experience and you say goodbye.

You feel yourself gently returning to your body feeling refreshed and happy from the visit to the special garden.

Chapter 8

Coping with Change

Children face so much change in their lives and new encounters on a daily basis. As adults we forget that our children are discovering everything for the first time, and just because we don't see something as being daunting doesn't mean that they see it through our experienced viewpoint. It's valuable to understand their viewpoint; but more than this, equipping them with the tools they need to cope with change is so important.

The guided meditations in this chapter are focused around the theme of change and helping children to embrace change as a natural process of life and not something they need to fear. Practicing the meditations will gently introduce your children to the concept of exploring the new with excitement and wonder which is so natural to them. Just because something is different or new doesn't mean it has to be avoided or seem scary.

Connecting with the Angels of transition and the energy of nature, your child will learn to embrace the new. You will also be working with a beautiful meditation to help children release worries and feelings of overwhelm in a safe and relaxing way.

Becoming one with nature

Being in nature is very healing and restorative. Children love to spend time outdoors running around and playing. At times, however, it isn't possible to spend time outside in nature, especially for those living in built-up areas or during winter when the evenings are dark early and the weather is cold. We can still tap into the healing and nurturing energy of nature, however, when we are not outdoors.

This meditation connects us to the healing powers of nature and is also beneficial in opening up creativity and becoming comfortable with transition and change. In reality everything is constantly changing; even our bodies are changing from day to day with new cells growing and old cells dying. We are never the same person from one minute to the next even though our perception may be different.

The ease in which nature accepts and is open to change is something that we can learn a great deal from. A tree never resists shedding its leaves for fear of losing itself in Autumn. It simply lets go and allows the wind to undress its branches. Similarly, a stream doesn't fight the rocks that stand in its path; it flows around or over them with ease, following a meandering route if necessary but nonetheless always moving, flowing and changing.

In order to become one with nature, let's experience it from a different perspective. Not as an outsider viewing it from afar, but from within, becoming part of nature. In reality we are not separate from nature or anything else as we are all the same, we are one.

Guided Meditation – Connecting with Nature
Good for: Connecting with nature, embracing change,
transition and grounding
Duration: 5 minutes
Best practiced: Anytime
Age Group: 3+

Begin by inviting in the energy of the elements:
"We call on the nurturing energy of the Earth, the powerful might of the Wind, the cleansing force of the Rain and the illuminating light of the Sun."

Take a deep breath in, and as you do, feel the caress of the breeze around your body, lifting you up and carrying you into the blue sky above.

As you float up with the breeze, you notice some fluffy white clouds above and around you, and as the wind blows the clouds, you realize that you are now also part of the clouds.

You no longer have a body, as you merge with the moist cloud formation that is speeding through the sky as the wind blows you along.

You feel free as a cloud being blown wherever the wind takes you, without a care or worry as to the direction or purpose of your route through the sky.

As you meet other clouds, you form a larger cloud and you feel their energy as you merge together.

Far below, you see fields and hills, flowers and rivers, and you know that soon you will fall to the earth as rain to join them.

As you become heavy with moisture you feel the mist coming together to form droplets.

As the cloud changes into rain, you feel yourself as a single raindrop but also as the body of rain falling through the air towards the earth.

Your descent makes you feel free and at the same time excited at the adventures that lie ahead.

As you arrive near the earth, you first hit the leaves of a tall tree, splashing from one leaf to the next as you drip further towards the ground.

You merge with other raindrops on the leaves as you splash and flow downwards.

Finally you reach the earth and the moist, welcoming soil absorbs you into its loving embrace.

As you blend into the soil, you become the earth and feel the nurturing, loving energy that it exudes.

You lie quietly for a while, enjoying this new energy that you are feeling.

Soon you feel yourself transforming once again.

You feel the power of the earth in you and flowing through you as you push your way upwards, realizing that you are growing, and as the dark soil gives way to light, you emerge as a tender plant into the world above; a tiny green stem that is growing and changing each day.

You enjoy the feeling of being rooted into the ground but also the sensation of the breeze blowing through your newly forming leaves and the heat of the sunlight on the leaves as they unfurl.

Nature loves you, supplying everything that you need, and you respond by growing strong and tall.

Each night you rest and each morning the warmth of the sun calls you to awaken and to prosper.

You drink in the warming sunlight and begin to grow beautiful flowers.

After the hot sunshine comes cooling rain and you cherish the feeling of the droplets splashing onto your leaves before being absorbed into the earth where your roots are. Drink up the moisture, and feel the rainwater flowing into your stem and leaves and flowers.

You again become the rain but in a different form now.

As the wind blows through your leaves, you feel yourself being lifted up once again into the sky, leaving behind the plant that you were and the earth, and floating gently upwards.

The wind brings you back to the present moment and you feel yourself returning to your body.

You keep your adventures with you and the powerful, transformative energy of the wind, earth, sun and rain.

When you feel ready, open your eyes.

Azrael – The Angel of Transition

Azrael the Angel of transition is always with you whenever you are going through big changes in your life, to help you sail through change and accept the new, but also to help you with small changes that you face every day.

Azrael wants you to know that change is good. It may sometimes feel uncomfortable at first, letting go of the familiar and facing something new, but the discomfort always passes and you learn to accept and look forward to positive changes in your life.

Azrael would like to take you on a journey to show you how change comes about and how it can lead to magnificent things.

Guided Meditation – The Angel of Transition
Good for: Ease, flow, transition and creativity
Duration: 5 minutes
Best practiced: Anytime
Age Group: 3+

"We call on Azrael the Angel of transition to be with us now."

Feel his loving energy surround you, wrapping you in his protective embrace.

Close your eyes and take his hand now as he guides you down a short path. At the end of the path is a set of steps, leading up into the sky. You climb the steps together, going up and up, higher and higher.

As you continue up, your head touches the clouds. You pass through the mist and arrive in a magical land where everything is so bright and colorful but very different than you are used to. Here there are winged unicorns flying through the sky, mermaids splashing and swimming in the sea, and Angels and fairies dancing and singing the most beautiful of songs.

The flowers glow brightly under the sun. The trees bear fruit, which you have never seen before, and the water is the most beautiful shade of blue.

There is so much magic to discover here and you feel very excited.

Then Azrael takes your hand and leads you to a fountain where you take a refreshing drink. You then sit down on a golden rock and Azrael speaks to you.

He tells you of the power of your imagination and how you can use it to imagine the life you want. He invites you to think about all the wonderful experiences that you'd like in your life and to have fun thinking about the happiness and enjoyment that they bring to you.

If you'd like more friends, see yourself surrounded by happy, supportive friends and having fun together.

If you'd like to feel healthy and well, see yourself full of health and feeling better than ever.

If you'd like to feel more loved, see and feel those you love most around you, hugging you and telling you how much they love you.

As you imagine and feel these experiences, you bring more of the same into your life.

Azrael tells you that you are very powerful, and you can be and do anything you wish.

He also tells you not to spend time worrying about things you don't want, just give your worries to the Angels. They will take them away if you ask.

Azrael shows you how this place which, if so different from what you know, is a very special place. You know this because you feel so welcome and loved here.

He explains, just because something is different it doesn't make it good or bad, it's just something new to discover. He wants you to have fun discovering and exploring everything new that you come across – new people, new places, new experiences. Ask the Angels to be with you and to help you explore the new.

Before you leave, you have some time to go explore this special place with Azrael. Take his hand and go see what there is to discover. Take your time and see where he takes you.

(Pause to allow them to explore!)

It's nearly time to leave. Azrael walks back with you to the steps that led you here.

Just before you go, take a final look around and wave to the animals and trees, and say goodbye.

Walking down the steps, you pass back through the clouds, back down and down until you finally reach the path.

Walk back down the path and come back into your body and the present moment.

Open your eyes when you're ready.

Guided Meditation – Letting go of Worry and Overwhelm
Good for: Release, peace, love and happiness
Duration: 5 minutes
Best practiced: Anytime
Age Group: 3+

Take a few deep breaths and close your eyes.

In your mind's eye, see yourself standing on a cliff top, facing out to the sea.

Admire the beauty and vastness of the ocean before you. It's a sunny day and in your hand you are holding a bunch of balloons.

What color are the balloons?

There is a gentle breeze and the balloons sway with the breeze as you hold the string in your hand.

You can now place inside each balloon something that is worrying you, something big or small that you have been holding onto and now need to let go of.

Imagine each thing that comes to mind being placed inside each of the balloons.

The more things that come up, the more balloons there are to place them into.

Spend as long as you want placing all your worries and concerns inside the balloons.

When you're ready, hold your hand up and let go of the string you have been holding onto. See the breeze take the balloons high up into the sky and out towards the ocean.

Watch as the balloons drift off and with them all your worries drift away also.

You feel much lighter now, much calmer and more peaceful. It's good to let go.

Know that whatever concerns you placed in the balloons are taken care of. They have been sent up to the heavens for the Angels to heal them.

There is nothing more you need to do.

Relax knowing all is well.

You are safe and supported. You are loved and protected. You are strong and powerful. You are perfect in every way.

The Angels see your perfection and want you to know this. They see your beauty and strength, and they love you so much.

Allow yourself to open up to receiving their love.

As you glance across the ocean, you see a beautiful rainbow appear in the sky and you smile, knowing this is a sign from the Angels.

In your own time reconnect with your body in the present moment and open your eyes.

Chapter 9

Mindful Activities

Body Language

Our body language has an important role to play in enhancing our mood. The proven physiological benefits of open, positive postures and expressions are something that we should take note of when it comes to expressing ourselves. When we consciously adopt open postures, we can enhance not only our mood but also the way in which others view us. American social psychologist Amy Cuddy has researched postures, which she calls "Power Poses." Expansive, open postures such as standing with arms outstretched and legs apart can be very powerful mood enhancers, but other benefits of these poses include increased self-esteem, confidence and positivity. A noted benefit of power poses is the reduction in the level of the stress hormone cortisol in our bodies and increased levels of the power hormone testosterone. Conversely, closed postures and negative facial expressions such as sitting with legs and arms crossed, back slumped and frowning can have the opposite effect, stress hormones increase, and not only do we feel less powerful and inferior, but others also view us in this way.

So what has this got to do with children and meditation? If we look at the natural posture of babies and toddlers when playing, they sit on the floor with back straight, and legs and arms open. It is rare to find a young child sitting with arms folded or back slouched. As we grow older, however, we tend to take on some closed postures, particularly when made to sit for prolonged periods such as when children start at school. While sitting at a desk is beneficial for the teacher to control and teach the class, it's not ideal for children who are used to moving about freely and frequently. The results of which can lead to slumping on desks, folded arms and legs, and other closed postures.

We can, however, encourage our little ones to draw on the psychological benefits of smiling and open postures by practicing them at home and encouraging their use in class.

Have fun with the following game to encourage positive open postures and facial expressions. Your child can then practice them during the day at school at break time or whenever they are feeling sad or angry to help enhance their mood!

Follow the Leader

You start off as the leader incorporating power poses and facial expressions, but after a while allow the child to be the leader and let them come up with their own poses. It doesn't matter if they are not in the ideal postures as long as they feel the game is interesting and fun, and they are taking an active part in it.

Explain the activity to the child, saying that you are the leader and they have to copy everything that you do.

1. Stand up straight with the arms outstretched above your body, now walk around on your tippy toes with arms still outstretched; while walking say wiggle your fingers, keep an eye on the children playing to make sure they are copying the actions.

2. Next, while walking around, place your hands on your hips, but stay on your tippy toes and tell the child to copy you.

3. Stop, stand on the spot and look at the ceiling/sky and raise your hands straight above your head, explaining what to do and asking the child to do the same.

4. Jump on the spot while in this position, then begin to jump around.

5. Stop jumping and stand very still, practice a few deep breaths before moving onto the next posture.

6. Next place your hands behind your head with elbows

stretched out to the sides, and feet hip distance apart; after a few seconds with the hands still behind the head try touching the elbows together before returning to the original pose with elbows out.

7. Do some jumping jacks on the spot.

8. If some older children are joining in ask if someone else wants to become the leader for a while.

9. Most of all have fun and enjoy coming up with new poses and actions to follow!

Lotus Position

When meditating, the posture we assume has an effect on the benefits of the meditation. The lotus position – sitting on the ground or a cushion, cross-legged – is a popular pose because of the benefits it offers. The body is relaxed but remains upright with the back straight. Blood flow to the brain is improved with the lower body compressed. A minimal amount of energy is used while in this posture. With the muscles relaxed, motor and sensory activity is decreased. As we don't have physical distractions in the lotus position, we allow a deeper meditative state to develop.

As children are often quite flexible, achieving the lotus position may be easier for them than for some adults. However, the goal isn't to sit in full lotus position for hours; the idea is to have fun stretching and moving the body before achieving stillness for a short period of meditation.

First practice gentle stretching movements such as those listed below. Never push the child to do more than they are able to and always keep the practice fun.

1. *Stand straight and bend the body forward at the hips, knees straight and touch your toes (or ankles or calves), remain here for a few breaths before returning to standing.*

2. *Sit on the floor with legs straight. Open the legs out wide, keeping the knees straight. First bend over towards the right leg, reaching out with the hands towards the foot and rest in this position for a few breaths. Return to an upright posture and repeat, this time stretching out towards the left leg.*

3. *Still sitting on the floor, bring the legs out straight in front of the body. Bend the knees and place the soles of the feet together, allowing the knees to fall open on either side. Place your hands around your feet and slowly bring the body forward, towards the feet, while keeping the back straight. Remain here for a few breaths before returning to your starting position.*

4. *Sitting on the floor with legs out straight, first bend your right knee and bring your right foot up towards your left thigh. Rest the foot on top of the upper thigh. Begin to bend the left knee, and with your hands, bring the left foot up towards the right thigh, resting the foot on top of the right thigh.*

Only go as far as is comfortable, and if there is any pain stop and return to a straight-legged position.

If flexibility doesn't allow for the feet to rest on top of the thighs, try resting just one foot on the thigh while keeping the other foot on the ground.

It may feel more natural to start with your left leg first and then bringing the right leg up on top of the left leg or vice versa. Try both ways to see which you prefer.

Pay Attention!

Children are bombarded with so many stimulating sights and sounds these days, it's no wonder that they can become distracted and lose focus. A trip to the shops may seem like a mundane activity to us but for children it can be quite overwhelming, particularly for extra sensitive children. There are bright lights, music, colorful displays and brands jumping out at us vying for our attention. The only way to cope is by blocking out the stimuli. Even at home their toys light up and make noises, which for a young child can be exciting but often overstimulating. Not to mention other electronic devices such as television, tablets and smartphones.

This exercise helps your child to develop observation and focus, tuning in to small details rather than tuning out.

---

1. Take one of their favorite toys or items. For younger children something simple like a teddy bear is perfect. Pick something with a bit more detail for older children.

2. Place the item in front of them and ask them to look at it for a few seconds taking in all the details of the object – the colors, shape, size, texture etc.

3. Now, ask them to close their eyes and recall the object in their mind, describing it to you. Allow them to describe as much detail as possible and then ask questions such as: "What color are the teddy bear's eyes?", or any other details that they might have missed.

4. Next, let the child reexamine the object, pointing out what they remembered and any additional details they might have missed. Be sure to do this in a loving manner saying, "Isn't it amazing how you see and hold teddy every day but you didn't realize what color his eyes are?"

5. If they enjoyed the process, try again with another item, gradually working up to more complex and detailed items. And be sure that everyone takes turns observing, including yourself!

With practice the exercise will help the child become more attentive, focused and improve concentration.

Inner Guide

One of the most empowering exercises that you can teach your child is to tune into and trust their own internal guidance – their intuition. When we learn to become mindful, we can easily tune into the body and its subtle indications, which are always guiding us. When we say that we have a "bad" feeling about something or a situation "doesn't feel right" this is our body's internal guidance, leading us away from danger or from a situation that doesn't serve us. So many of us have lost touch with this natural guidance, however, and rather than going within for guidance, we look outside of ourselves to other people, the Internet, books or any number of other things to seek advice. If we can learn to re-attune to our own inner guide, which always has our best interest at heart, we can make instant decisions for our best interest and the best interest of all involved. Wouldn't it be wonderful to teach your child how to do this and to use their intuition daily? This simple, effective exercise will help to bring focus and attention back to the body, and to become aware of its guidance.

Let's Sway

This method of muscle testing is a quick, simple and effective way to tune into the body. It's a great way to get a "yes" or "no" indication when asking a question.

1. Begin by determining which direction your body sways to indicate Yes and which direction for No. Most people lean forward for Yes and back for No, but for some people it's the opposite. No motion – remaining still – or circular motion indicates that the answer is uncertain. If so, trust that the answer will be indicated another time when it's right for you.

2. Standing tall and straight with feet flat on the floor, hip distance apart and hands by your sides, ask your child to become still. Explain how the exercise works. Start off asking some questions that you know the answer to, such as, "Is my name Sandra?" Always ask questions where the answer is Yes or No. Then allow your body to sway slightly forwards or backwards. A forward motion usually indicates Yes and a backward motion usually indicates No.

3. Ask a few questions where you already know the answer, using both Yes and No responses first to practice. Then ask a question where you don't know the answer. Start off with simple questions such as, "Should I have eggs for breakfast?" and so on. Practiced enough, your child will learn to use this exercise to guide them in other decisions, learning to trust their intuition.

Remember, however, that there may be times where their intuitive guidance can be interpreted incorrectly. Always take the exercise with a light heart.

Chapter 10

Bedtime

Often when going to bed we are not yet ready to sleep, our minds are still active, our muscles are primed for action and we need some time to release thoughts and relax our bodies. Children in particular can need help relaxing before bed, especially if they are still in action mode before sleep. Often they need to use up excess energy before going to sleep, which is good to tire them out, but after a bout of play and excitement they can find it hard to switch off.

This meditation will help to ease them into a relaxed state and prepare their bodies and minds for sleep.

During the day our bodies do so much work that we are not even aware of. Our heart beats, pumping blood and oxygen to our muscles and organs. Our muscles are constantly being used to help us to walk, run, and move. Our lungs are expanding and contracting as we breathe, taking in oxygen and breathing out carbon dioxide. Our digestive systems are absorbing nutrients from our food and converting food into energy. All this happens often without us even being aware of the work that our bodies are doing in each moment.

Let's take some time to thank our body for all the functions it performs and allow the body to relax.

Guided Meditation – Giving Thanks for Your Body
Good for: Self-confidence, appreciation, relaxation, health and well-being
Duration: 10 minutes
Best practiced: Anytime
Age Group: 4+

Close your eyes and take a few deep breaths.

Concentrate on your feet saying, "Thank you, feet, for helping me to balance, walk and run today, and everything else that you do for me. You can now relax. I love you."

Feel any tension being released from your feet.

Sense your ankles and say, "Thank you, ankles, for helping me to use my feet and to dance, play, and everything else that you do for me. You can now relax. I love you."

Feel any tension being released from your ankles.

Focus on your lower legs and calves saying, "Thank you, legs, for helping me to stand, sit and jump, and everything else that you do for me. You can now relax. I love you."

Feel any tension being released from your lower legs.

Bring your attention to your knees and say, "Thank you, knees, for helping me to kneel, bend my legs, skip and everything else that you do for me. You can now relax. I love you."

Feel any tension being released from your knees.

Sense your thighs and say, "Thank you, thighs, for helping me to sprint, climb, cycle and everything else that you do for me. You can now relax. I love you."

Feel any tension being released from your thighs.

Focus on your hips saying, "Thank you, hips, for helping me to bend, stretch, tumble and everything else that you do for me. You can now relax. I love you."

Feel any tension being released from your hips.

Bring your attention to your tummy and say, "Thank you, tummy, for helping me to digest my food and create energy, and everything else that you do for me. You can now relax. I love you."

Feel any tension being released from your tummy.

Concentrate on your lower back saying, "Thank you, lower back, for helping me to be flexible, to support my body and posture, and everything else that you do for me. You can now relax. I love you."

Feel any tension being released from your lower back.

Focus on your chest, heart and lungs saying, "Thank you, chest, heart and lungs, for helping me to breathe, to create energy and everything else that you do for me. You can now relax. I love you."

Feel any tension being released from your chest, heart and lungs.

Sense your upper back and say, "Thank you, upper back, for helping me to stand tall and straight, to twist and bend, and everything else that you do for me. You can now relax. I love you."

Feel any tension being released from your upper back.

Bring your attention to your shoulders, arms, elbows and hands and say, "Thank you, shoulders, arms, elbows and hands, for helping me with my coordination and movement, to lift and throw, and everything else that you do for me. You can now relax. I love you."

Feel any tension being released from your shoulders, arms, elbows and hands.

Focus on your throat and neck saying, "Thank you, throat and neck, for helping me to breathe, talk, move my head and everything else that you do for me. You can now relax. I love you."

Feel any tension being released from your throat and neck.

Sense your face and head and say, "Thank you, face and head, for helping me to eat, breathe, see, smile, talk, think, hear, to express myself and everything else that you do for me. You can now relax. I love you."

Feel any tension being released from your face and head.

Finally, bring your attention to your whole body, thanking all the other parts and organs saying, "Thank you to every part of my body for all the work that you do. You can now relax. I love you."

Finish by taking a few deep breaths.

Note: Your child may fall asleep before you finish this relaxing meditation with them; continue on reading to them, as they will still receive the benefit as they sleep.

If questions come up during the meditation about the body and its functions, use the time to explain to your child about what happens and help them to appreciate their body and all that it does.

Loving their body promotes positive self-awareness, self-appreciation, confidence and self-love.

Guided Meditation – Angels of Sleep
Good for: Relaxation, sleep, imagination and healing
Duration: 15 minutes
Best practiced: Bedtime
Age Group: 3+

"We ask for our Healing Angels and the Angels of sleep to be here and to connect with us now."

The Healing Angels and the Angels of sleep and rest are by your side and also surrounding you.

You feel very comfortable with them, and you feel relaxed and peaceful.

The Angels show you a wonderful bed that is so big you need a ladder to climb up onto it.

Climbing the ladder onto the bed, you see beautiful colored pillows and cushions, and the most wonderful soft blankets of every color.

As you lie on the bed you seem to sink into the comfortable warm blankets, and they feel soft and welcoming as they touch your skin.

The Angels of sleep tell you that they want to tell you a story. They want to tell you about what happens when you go to sleep...

They begin by telling you that you are always protected by your Guardian Angel, even while you sleep, and that they are always by your side.

You never need to be worried or afraid of the dark or of the night, as the Angels are there to protect you and to light your way, even if you can't see them.

They tell you that if ever you feel afraid that you just need to ask them for their help and they will be there for you.

You can ask for them to let you know they are with you through a feeling, and if you wait quietly you will feel a sense of love and warmth or tingling from them.

The Angels tell you that it is very important to sleep and to rest as it is the time when your body grows and heals, but it is also the time that you go to meet your Angels through your dreams.

If you have a question or something that is worrying you, you can ask your Angels for the answer before you go to sleep and they will give you the answer in a dream.

You can also ask for them to help you to remember that dream when you wake up.

You can ask them a question now if you would like to...

The Angels of sleep want to show you some of the beautiful places that you go to when you sleep, and as they take you by the hand you see yourself flying up into the starry night sky.

You feel safe and happy that they are going to show you such beautiful things.

As you look back, you see the whole world from above, and you are surprised and delighted at the beauty of it.

You fly through space and you pass many stars along the way.

Suddenly a planet comes into view just ahead of you.

Your Angel tells you that this is a very special place that you are about to visit.

As you pass through white fluffy clouds, you see the beautiful blue sky all around you.

Just ahead, you see a huge rainbow of every color.

As you fly closer to the rainbow the colors become stronger and brighter.

Just before you reach the rainbow, you pass through a mist of light rain that tickles your face as you fly through it.

You finally reach the rainbow and you fly through each of its colors, first red, then orange, followed by yellow, green, blue, indigo, purple and white.

You smile at the Angel holding your hand and feel happy to be in this beautiful place.

As you float through the sky you look down and see a beautiful green field, filled with flowers.

As the field gets closer, you and your Angel land on the soft grass and you feel the cool earth beneath your feet.

Looking around, you see a beautiful waterfall nearby. The

sunlight catches and sparkles in the flowing water.

You walk over to the waterfall and you feel the spray of water gently touching your skin.

You dip your feet into the pool below the waterfall and the clear water feels nice as it flows around your feet.

You decide to sit here for a moment in this special place, relaxing and feeling the warmth of the sun on your face and body.

Your Angel tells you that it is time to go and as they take your hand once again, the two of you fly off into the sky.

As you float through the air, you feel relaxed and sleepy.

Your Angel is taking you back to that wonderful, cozy, big bed.

In the blink of an eye, you feel yourself being lowered down onto the bed and you snuggle up in the warmth of the blankets, closing your eyes.

The Angels of sleep stay with you while you drift off to sleep and you thank them for the wonderful experience.

As you drift into a deep, relaxing sleep, the Angels shower you with blessings.

Chapter 11

Meditation for Parents

Forgiveness

Part of our children's purpose, amongst others, is to be our teachers, to help us to learn and to grow. We might think that as parents it is our role to teach and guide our little ones, and while this is true to an extent, we learn some of our greatest lessons from our children. We can become so enmeshed, however, in the role of parent, ruler, enforcer that when our children go against our will we can become very frustrated. We have two options in this case: we can try to enforce our will with greater effort or we can release control and allow our children to guide us, with the exception of circumstances that are dangerous or potentially harmful, of course.

We also need to judge when to release control and when our children are testing our boundaries, and we need to stick to our conviction – it's a fine line!

Quite often, when this clash of will occurs frequently it can lead to anger, frustration and weariness. We can blame our children for "acting up" or misbehaving when all the time we've been missing the lesson they are trying to teach us. For me, one of the lessons I am learning is patience; other predominant lessons can be acceptance, letting go, mindfulness, attentiveness, tolerance and unconditional love. However, we completely miss the learning opportunity when we become embroiled in anger, blame and unforgiveness.

It sounds strange that we could bear a grudge against our children but sometimes, often subconsciously, we hold unforgiveness in our hearts.

Healing this emotional pain and letting go is the key to opening up to unconditional love. When we love our children in this way, small grievances no longer take hold of us and we become more patient, loving, understanding parents and create a more loving environment for our children to grow and prosper. We also allow ourselves to integrate any lessons that come up with greater ease and acceptance.

The following meditation helps us to release any hurt that we may be holding onto, and allows us to forgive our children for any perceived wrongdoings and to move forward in peace.

Guided Meditation – Forgiveness

Begin by sitting in a comfortable position and close your eyes.

Take a moment to relax your body, taking a few long, deep breaths.

Ask the Angels to be by your side saying, "I now ask for the assistance of my Guardian Angel and the Angel Phanuel."

Bring your focus of attention to your heart. Spend a moment connecting with your heart, allowing any emotions that come up to be recognized and felt.

"Angel Phanuel, please place your healing hands over my heart." See the Angel reaching out and holding her hands in front of your chest and at your back.

"I now ask for any hurt and unforgiveness in relation to [Name(s)] to be healed and released."

See the Angel's hands lighting up and glowing with a beautiful golden, white light. Feel her reaching into your heart center, and very gently healing and removing any pain that resides here.

Allow yourself to let go.

Spend a few moments in quiet meditation while Phanuel works away, healing and balancing your heart. Feel the release this brings, like a weight has been lifted from you.

When ready, ask Phanuel to heal other areas of your body, saying, "Phanuel, please heal any other areas connected to my heart where I am holding pain and unforgiveness that need to be released."

As Phanuel works at healing and releasing these pent-up emotions, connect with your body and sense what areas are coming up, and consciously allow yourself to let go.

Spend as long as you want sitting in meditation as Phanuel goes about her work.

When ready, ask your Guardian Angel to seal your aura with protective light, "Guardian Angel, please place a golden seal of protective light around me now to protect my energy."

Allow yourself to come back to the present moment and gently open your eyes.

Thank the Angels for their help.

Note: As this meditation can be very powerful, it can bring up strong emotions. Be aware of how you feel afterwards; and if emotions come to the surface for release, allow them to flow through you rather than pushing them back down or wallowing in them.

Emotional Balance

We all know of the energy field or aura that surrounds our body. In fact, it is our physical body that resides inside our aura, a bit like an egg yolk that resides inside the egg. Similar to an egg, which has many levels i.e. the yolk, the white, the skin and the shell, our energy fields are also made up of layers – the physical, mental, emotional and spiritual. Each level operates in tandem, and if one is out of balance, the other levels also become unbalanced.

The following meditation is a simple and effective way of

restoring harmony to each part of our being.

Guided Meditation – Emotional Balance

"I ask for the Angel of Divine Balance – Dokiel – and my Divine Angelic team of light to connect with me now."

Allow the peaceful, loving energies of Angel Dokiel to wrap around you and to hold you in his loving embrace.

"I ask for the Angels to build up my body and mind with the energy of patience and love."

See the Angels holding out their hands, and see the pure white light of patience and love coming from their hands towards you.

Feel the light as it enters your body and begins to fill your entire being with the peaceful, relaxing energies.

Feel each and every cell, every particle of your body filling with this light.

Allow a moment for the light to build up in your system.

Once your physical body has filled up with this light, it begins to overflow into the next level of your energy field – your emotional body, surrounding and connected to your physical body.

Allow the light to build up and to immerse your emotional body with the loving energies.

As your emotional energy body absorbs the light, it now begins to overflow into your mental body surrounding and connected to your emotional body.

Feel the waves of peace and joy as they fill up your mental body with their healing energies, allowing you to let go of heavy mental energy as this loving light replaces it.

As the waves of positive mental energy fill up and overflow from your being, the energy now pours into your spiritual body

> and it begins to glow with the light of patience, love and under-standing.
>
> Allow a moment for this energy to build up within your energetic spiritual body.
>
> You are now healed and revitalized on a physical, emotional, mental and spiritual level.
>
> Ask the Angels to seal this light into each level of your being and to place an outer golden sphere of protection around you now.
>
> Picture yourself inside a shiny golden egg of protection.
>
> Thank the Angels for their assistance.
>
> When you are ready open your eyes.

Guided Meditation – Understanding

> Sit in a comfortable position and close your eyes.
>
> "I ask the Angels of divine patience and understanding to be present and to connect with me now."
>
> "I ask the Angels to very gently enter my aura to heal, dissolve and remove any blockages in my system that may be preventing me from being a patient, loving and understanding parent."
>
> Allow a few minutes for the Angels to work away, clearing your system of any emotional energy that no longer serves you and that needs to be released.
>
> Take a few deep breaths and just be conscious with each out-breath of letting go (there is no need to be aware on a conscious level of what is coming up for release, just be aware of letting go of whatever needs to be released).
>
> When you feel ready, ask the Angels to fill your being with

healing energies to replace any latent energy that has been released.

Feel your system filling up with healing, loving light, revitalizing your entire being.

Allow a moment for your energy system to soak up these energies.

Your Angels tell you to picture your child or children in front of you. See them smiling and happy.

Feel the love that you have for them in your heart. Allow this loving sensation to build up until it is overflowing from your being.

Send this abundant love to your child.

See the loving energies flowing from your heart (you may picture this energy as beautiful pink swirls of light emanating from your chest).

See the pink loving light swirl all around your child, filling them with your pure love.

See their faces fill with joy as they accept and appreciate this love that you are sending to them.

As the love flows from your heart it continues to grow stronger and flow more easily.

You see the heart of your child opening up, and they send pink loving swirls of light back to you.

You gratefully accept the love that they are sending and you open your heart to receive.

As the flow of love and light passes between you, it continues to grow even stronger.

Your Angels place a sphere of protective energy around both you and your child to preserve and to protect the love between you.

Thank the Angels for their help and for this wonderful experience.

Feel yourself gradually returning to your body and to the present moment.

When you feel ready, open your eyes.

Chapter 12

Angel Prayers and Invocations

Use the following Angelic invocations and prayers to call on the Angels to help with a particular issue or simply to feel their loving presence around you and your child. Saying the prayers and calling on the Angels together each day helps your child to learn how to ask the Angels for help, and to know that their Angelic helpers are always at hand for any need.

Protection

This prayer or invocation is a lovely way to set your children up energetically for the day. It is particularly useful if they are heading off to school where they are interacting with many other people. The purpose of this prayer is to provide energetic protection so that only loving, positive energy can reach your child, keeping them protected from negative energy. Of course, this isn't a form of physical protection; it is spiritual protection for their energy system, helping to keep them energetically balanced and positively aligned.

It also helps to prevent their energy from being drawn on by others. If you have ever encountered a person that left you feeling drained and tired, you'll know what I mean. Some people – most of the time subconsciously – can draw on others' energy for their own needs instead of connecting to universal life force energy or energy from source. When we practice regular energetic protection it prevents others from depleting our energy while also keeping our energy positive and light.

If your child is particularly sensitive, this practice is a must for them; however, I would recommend that it is also done for all children whether going to school or not, to help keep their energy field protected and balanced.

At the start of the day recite this prayer with your child. If they are old enough to visualize, they can close their eyes and envision the protective cloak around them as they say the prayer. If a child is too young to say the prayer, you can say it on their behalf.

Invoking Angelic Protection

"I ask Archangel Michael and the Angels of divine protection to be with me now. I ask for the divine cloak of protection of Archangel Michael to be placed around me, covering and protecting every part of me. I am now wrapped in the safety and love of Archangel Michael. I feel safe, protected and supported."

Note: The cloak is traditionally cobalt blue in color; however, your child may envision another color that is right for them. Indeed, the color of the cloak may change over time depending on their needs. If they are visualizing the cloak around them, ask them what color it is!

Archangel Michael can also be asked to place his protective cloak around objects and belongings to provide protection if so desired.

Angelic Healing with Archangel Raphael

"Archangel Raphael, Archangel Raphael, Archangel Raphael, please be present now and connect with me, placing your healing hands on me, providing whatever healing energy that I most need now."

Take a few deep breaths and feel any changes in the energy around you. Allow yourself to receive the healing energy by stating, "I am open to receiving the healing that Archangel Raphael and the Healing Angels are now offering."

Allow yourself to relax and to receive.

Inner Peace & Tranquility

"Archangel Uriel, Archangel Uriel, Archangel Uriel, please be with me now. Enfold me in your wings of light and bring me the peace and tranquility that I so desire. I place all my trust in you."

Take a few deep-relaxing breaths and feel the loving presence of Archangel Uriel as he holds you in his protective embrace.

Tip: Say this with your child as they go asleep and ask Uriel to hold them in his loving wings throughout the night.

Angelic Guidance

"Archangel Gabriel, Archangel Gabriel, Archangel Gabriel, guide me now in my thoughts, words and deeds. Help me to make clear, divinely guided decisions at the right time and for the highest good of all concerned."

Morning Prayer

Every day I shine a light
from my heart
it shines so bright.
It lights the path ahead for me
and everyone I meet and see.
I shine a light of gold and white,
of silver and of purple too.
All the colors of the rainbow
fill my aura with their hue.

Bedtime Prayer

Now we go to a quiet place
where dreams come true and our souls awake.
Now we rest, it's time for sleep,
a sleep so comforting and deep.
Our soft, cozy bed that we lie upon,
we stay protected, safe and warm.
Close your eyes and rest, my dear,
do not worry, let go of fears.
Mommy and Daddy are always here.
In your heart our love resides,
as we sit with you by your bedside.
We bless your head and your heart,
and seal in our love while we're apart.
For there is no distance between us and you,
because our love is inside you too.

Conclusion

My first experience of meditation as a child was during a school retreat where we experienced a guided meditation. During the meditation we visualized meeting a guide who gave each of us a gift. I saw my gift clearly in my mind's eye: it was an amber stone necklace. I was so amazed that I could clearly see this gift and it seemed so special to me. It had a profound and lasting effect. It wasn't until many years later, however, that I began to study meditation and adopt a regular practice.

I've come across so many stories of children who have benefitted from practicing meditation and I wanted to finish by sharing a few of these stories with you. Beginning with my own son who is now three, I have introduced him to the practice of meditation in a gentle way. We practice deep breathing and visualizing regularly but only if he wants to. I never try to force the practice on him. Often after I have read a story going to bed, we'll turn out the lights and he'll lie down and ask me to do color Angels. We'll work through the chakras, breathing in each color as we go and he'll settle down to sleep afterwards. It's a lovely way to end the day and a great way to let go of emotions and energy that have built up, and allow him to "reset" before drifting off to sleep.

Teaching teenagers meditation, it gives me such pleasure to see the noticeable difference in their demeanor when they enter the classroom and when they leave only forty minutes later. They begin the class in a rather restless, unfocused state, and invariably leave with a subdued, calm, relaxed demeanor.

Many students approach their first meditation class with eager anticipation, while others come to class with trepidation, not knowing what to expect. One such student, let's call her Sarah, arrived at her first class and I immediately sensed her unwillingness to take part. Her body language spoke volumes as she spent the entire class with legs and arms crossed, and expressed her disinterest by occasionally biting her fingernails, while the other students listened attentively and actively took part in the meditation practices. Even though everyone else closed their eyes to enjoy the meditations, Sarah kept her eyes open throughout. I sensed her fear and while I knew that she – of all the students – needed this the most, I would never force any of the students to take part. Indeed, I had expressed this at the start of the class letting the students know that they didn't have to do the meditation practices if they didn't want to. I prefer to let them explore the practice in their own time when they feel ready.

The following week, I taught the same class and I wondered how Sarah would react during her second meditation class. Normally the students are more open to the second class, as they now know what to expect and they have enjoyed our first session together. The students walked in and sat down. I explained what we were going to be practicing during the class. As they closed their eyes to begin their first meditation I glanced over at Sarah and happily noted her serene state – eyes closed, hands relaxed in her lap and both feet on the floor. It was like a different person. For the rest of the class she remained calm, attentive and engaged. As the class ended I overheard her whisper to a friend, "That was so relaxing." And while such transformations are not always as pronounced, there is always a greater sense of peace and calm amongst the students at the end of each class.

As part of her MindUP program, Goldie Hawn has brought mindfulness into the classroom with some 650,000 students having taken part so far. She describes one experience of a boy with autism who was about to take an exam. The thoughts of the exam had caused him such distress that he was physically shaking. Another boy in the class spotted this and asked the teacher if they could do their breathing break first, rather than starting the exam straight away. The teacher agreed, and afterwards the boy had stopped shaking and calmed down enough to take the exam. How wonderful is this story? It shows not just the beneficial effects of meditation for relieving stress but also how it brings greater empathy and compassion into the classroom. It also gives the students the tools they need to deal with stress, almost instantly in some cases.

My intention isn't just to introduce children to meditation, however, as a nice way to relax, although it sure beats other methods of "relaxation" such as television. I intend to give my sons and all the children I teach the tools they need to navigate life, to enable them to embrace their emotions and to know what to do if feeling angry or despondent or overwhelmed. I want to set them up for self-mastery, and in so doing be a shining light unto others, enabling them to light the way ahead. I want to give them something much more than breathing techniques; I want to give them awareness, to really live life, embracing all its wonderful possibilities rather than just going through the motions as so many do.

And this is what I wish for everyone who reads this book – that the processes will open you and your children up to something much larger than relaxation, although this in itself is a wonderful gift. Even if only for a moment, in their discovery of the Angels and meditation and all that they have to offer, your children glimpse the vastness of possibility and the potential they hold, they will have found much more than a way in which to relax; they will have found life, and that is worthy of your commitment to introducing and practicing meditation with them. After all, meditation is such an insignificant word to describe all that this amazing practice has to offer. It is a gift that you can offer to your children that will continue to give and give, if they so wish.

Be amazing my dear friends.

Namaste,

Sandra

Acknowledgments

I offer so much love and gratitude to the Angels for guiding my writing and gifting me with the beautiful meditations in this book. To you, the reader, I thank you from my heart for following your Angel's guidance, for reading this book and teaching the practices to the children in your life. The world is becoming a better place because of you.

A down pouring of love and gratitude to my family – my parents, my sister and brother-in-law, my husband and sons whose constant love and support fills my days with joy.

A special thanks to Rebecca, Abbie and Nathan who were my first inspiration for writing this book.

Thanks also to the team at John Hunt Publishing for their belief in this book and their wonderful efforts to help my dream become a reality.

Finally, to all those, through their generosity, kindness, inspiration and support, who helped in some way, big or small, to make this book possible, thank you, thank you, thank you.

About the Author

Sandra Rea is a spiritual teacher, author and energy healer. She helps people to release limiting thoughts and behavior that is holding them back and reconnect with the highest divine expression of themselves. Through her courses and lectures, she shares her wisdom and knowledge to allow people to break free from the chains of imagined limits and start living a life of freedom and possibility. She lives in Ireland where she spends her days doing the work that she loves, meditating and having fun with her children.

BOOKS

O-BOOKS

SPIRITUALITY

O is a symbol of the world, of oneness and unity; this eye represents knowledge and insight. We publish titles on general spirituality and living a spiritual life. We aim to inform and help you on your own journey in this life. If you have enjoyed this book, why not tell other readers by posting a review on your preferred book site? Recent bestsellers from O-Books are:

Heart of Tantric Sex
Diana Richardson
Revealing Eastern secrets of deep love and intimacy to Western couples.
Paperback: 978-1-90381-637-0 ebook: 978-1-84694-637-0

Crystal Prescriptions
The A-Z guide to over 1,200 symptoms and their healing crystals
Judy Hall
The first in the popular series of four books, this handy little guide is packed as tight as a pill-bottle with crystal remedies for ailments.
Paperback: 978-1-90504-740-6 ebook: 978-1-84694-629-5

Take Me To Truth
Undoing the Ego
Nouk Sanchez, Tomas Vieira
The best-selling step-by-step book on shedding the Ego, using
the teachings of *A Course In Miracles*.
Paperback: 978-1-84694-050-7 ebook: 978-1-84694-654-7

The 7 Myths about Love...Actually!
The journey from your HEAD to the HEART of your SOUL
Mike George
Smashes all the myths about LOVE.
Paperback: 978-1-84694-288-4 ebook: 978-1-84694-682-0

The Holy Spirit's Interpretation of the New Testament
A course in Understanding and Acceptance
Regina Dawn Akers
Following on from the strength of *A Course in Miracles*, NTI
teaches us how to experience the love and oneness of God.
Paperback: 978-1-84694-085-9 ebook: 978-1-78099-083-5

The Message of A Course In Miracles
A translation of the text in plain language
Elizabeth A. Cronkhite
A translation of *A Course in Miracles* into plain, everyday
language for anyone seeking inner peace. The companion
volume, Practicing a Course In Miracles, offers practical lessons
and mentoring.
Paperback: 978-1-84694-319-5 ebook: 978-1-84694-642-4

Rising in Love
My Wild and Crazy Ride to Here and Now, with Amma, the
Hugging Saint
Ram Das Batchelder
Rising in Love conveys an author's extraordinary journey of

spiritual awakening with the Guru, Amma.
Paperback: 978-1-78279-687-9 ebook: 978-1-78279-686-2

Thinker's Guide to God
Peter Vardy
An introduction to key issues in the philosophy of religion.
Paperback: 978-1-90381-622-6

Your Simple Path
Find happiness in every step
Ian Tucker
A guide to helping us reconnect with what is really important in our lives.
Paperback: 978-1-78279-349-6 ebook: 978-1-78279-348-9

365 Days of Wisdom
Daily Messages To Inspire You Through The Year
Dadi Janki
Daily messages which cool the mind, warm the heart and guide you along your journey.
Paperback: 978-1-84694-863-3 ebook: 978-1-84694-864-0

Body of Wisdom
Women's Spiritual Power and How it Serves
Hilary Hart
Bringing together the dreams and experiences of women across the world with today's most visionary spiritual teachers.
Paperback: 978-1-78099-696-7 ebook: 978-1-78099-695-0

Dying to Be Free
From Enforced Secrecy to Near Death to True Transformation
Hannah Robinson
After an unexpected accident and near-death experience,
Hannah Robinson found herself radically transforming her life,

while a remarkable new insight altered her relationship with
her father; a practising Catholic priest.
Paperback: 978-1-78535-254-6 ebook: 978-1-78535-255-3

The Ecology of the Soul
A Manual of Peace, Power and Personal Growth for Real People
in the Real World
Aidan Walker
Balance your own inner Ecology of the Soul to regain your
natural state of peace, power and wellbeing.
Paperback: 978-1-78279-850-7 ebook: 978-1-78279-849-1

Not I, Not other than I
The Life and Teachings of Russel Williams
Steve Taylor, Russel Williams
The miraculous life and inspiring teachings of one of the
World's greatest living Sages.
Paperback: 978-1-78279-729-6 ebook: 978-1-78279-728-9

On the Other Side of Love
A woman's Unconventional Journey Towards Wisdom
Muriel Maufroy
When life has lost all meaning, what do you do?
Paperback: 978-1-78535-281-2 ebook: 978-1-78535-282-9

Practicing A Course In Miracles
A Translation of the Workbook in Plain Language and With
Mentoring Notes
Elizabeth A. Cronkhite
The practical second and third volumes of The Plain-Language
A Course in Miracles.
Paperback: 978-1-84694-403-1 ebook: 978-1-78099-072-9

Quantum Bliss
The Quantum Mechanics of Happiness, Abundance, and Health
George S. Mentz
Quantum Bliss is the breakthrough summary of success and
spirituality secrets that customers have been waiting for.
Paperback: 978-1-78535-203-4 ebook: 978-1-78535-204-1

The Upside Down Mountain
Mags MacKean
A must-read for anyone weary of chasing success and happiness
– one woman's inspirational journey swapping the uphill slog
for the downhill slope.
Paperback: 978-1-78535-171-6 ebook: 978-1-78535-172-3

Your Personal Tuning Fork
The Endocrine System
Deborah Bates
Discover your body's health secret, the endocrine system, and
'twang' your way to sustainable health!
Paperback: 978-1-84694-503-8 ebook: 978-1-78099-697-4

Readers of ebooks can buy or view any of these
bestsellers by clicking on the live link in the title. Most
titles are published in paperback and as an ebook.
Paperbacks are available in traditional bookshops. Both
print and ebook formats are available online.

Find more titles and sign up to our readers' newsletter at
http://www.johnhuntpublishing.com/mind-body-spirit
Follow us on Facebook at
https://www.facebook.com/OBooks/
and Twitter at https://twitter.com/obooks